THE SCIENCE OF PALMISTRY AND ITS RELATIONS TO ASTROLOGY AND PHRENOLOGY

THE SCIENCE OF PALMISTRY AND ITS RELATIONS TO ASTROLOGY AND PHRENOLOGY

BY

IRENE SMITH

GYAN

Published by

GYAN

Gyan Publishing House
5, Ansari Road
Daryaganj, New Delhi-110002
Phone: 011-47034999, 9811692060
E-mail: books@gyanbooks.com

Distribution Network
gyanbooks.com
India, USA, Canada, UK, Australia, France

ISBN : 978-81-212-2089-7 (PB)
First Published, 1901

2nd Impression 2021

Printed at: Gyan Press, Delhi.

The Science of Palmistry and its Relations to Astrology and Phrenology
Author: Irene Smith

THE SCIENCE OF PALMISTRY

AND ITS RELATIONS TO ASTROLOGY AND PHRENOLOGY

✠ ✠

BY IRENE SMITH

✠ ✠

PUBLISHED BY
IRENE SMITH
P. O. BOX 945 TACOMA, WASH.

Yours Fraternally
Mrs. Irene Smith

Dedication.

To all brave souls who are seeking to solve the riddle of life, and thereby build up a higher civilization, do I lovingly dedicate this work of my heart, head and hand, hoping it will meet with your kind approval, and be of the same value to you it has been to me.

CONTENTS.

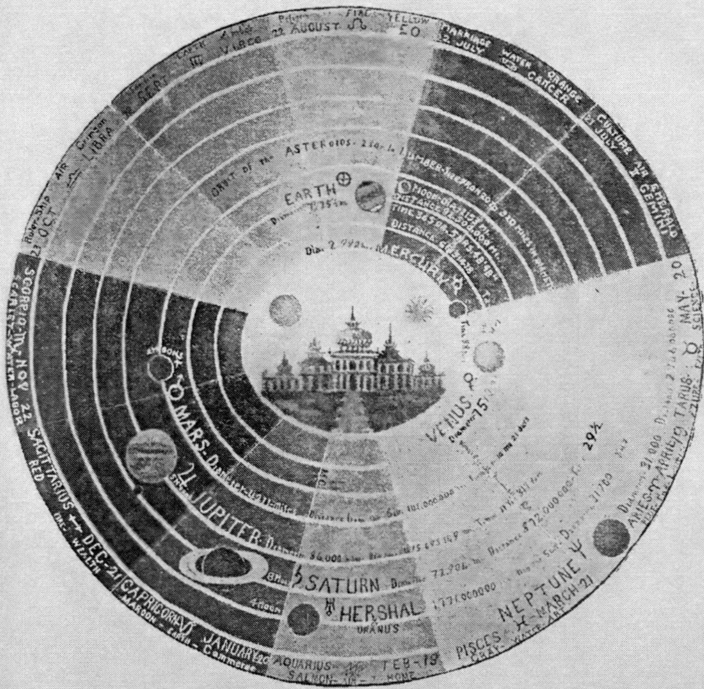

PLATE No. 1—*THE ZODIAC.*

The Temple in center of Zodiac is a Symbol of the New Institutions of the Future based on the Twelve Laws of Man's Nature.

THE SCIENCE OF PALMISTRY

AND ITS RELATIONS TO

ASTROLOGY AND PHRENOLOGY.

CHAPTER I.

Introduction.

In introducing this book to the public, it is with the view of illustrating the beautiful relation the sciences of astrology, phrenology and palmistry bear to one another, and their combined influence upon life. The great need of the day is a simple yet comprehensive system of character reading. Our parents and teachers are all in the dark in regard to the disposition and general qualities of the child, and more often than otherwise they administer the wrong training, to the great disadvantage of the child, as well as society. Now, after four years steady application of the above sciences, where I have read carefully about eight thousand people, I feel prepared to give to the world a new book, wherein I will endeavor to show in simple, plain terms, the advantage to be derived from a thorough knowledge, on the part of all the people, of the above sciences.

The first in order is astrology. I shall not attempt to teach in this small work astrology in full, only so far as it is of every day use to the student, in the still greater science of palmistry, which I will treat in full in this present manual. To those who wish to still further investigate astrology I should recommend such works as Butler's Solar Biology and Eleanor Kirk's works; which, so far as the Signs of the Zodiac are concerned, are very correct, as a rule. At least, I have found them so. I speak especially of these two works, as they have been of such value to me in my investigation along the line of astrology. If one wishes to study still further, Merton's Heliocentric Astrology, a modern, up to date work, is worth your attention. The standard works on astrology for the purpose of casting horoscopes are Raphael or Zadkiel.

Now, with this slight introduction, I will begin my own work, hoping it will meet with your approval, and will be of the same value to you that it has been to me, in helping you to broaden out in all lines of thought, and to understand and appreciate more fully, yourself and fellow men.

CHAPTER II.

What Are the Signs of the Zodiac?

In the study of Astrology, the first thing the student should do is to learn thoroughly the Signs of the Zodiac; what they are, and what these magnetic forces produce upon human life. What is a Sign of the Zodiac? I have met many people who have asked me that question; so, for fear some may still not know, I will explain, our Solar System, drawn on an ellipse as you will see in engraving No. 1, represents our suns and their family of planets.

Now you notice this ellipse is divided into twelve equal parts; the planets circling around the sun each in its own orbit, comes periodically in magnetic contact, with twelve other solar systems in making its orbit once around the sun. Take our own earth for example; it makes its orbit once in 365 days, which we divide into twelve months, which we call one year. So this very Astrology, or, as it is now called, Astronomy, divides up our time, giving us our days, months and year, according to the movements of these heavenly bodies. We are in but the infancy of the growth of this science. We are as a people, but slightly conscious as yet of the value Astrology and Astronomy will be to the race. We must remember we are just recovering from the deluge of darkness the world was plunged into during the so-called dark ages; when, for over a thousand years, ignorance reigned supreme. During this period the beautiful sciences were relegated to oblivion, as it was considered wicked to reason or think for one's self. But those times, dear reader, are past. We have come to the Age of Reason; have passed well through it, and the glimmer of a still more beautiful age is seen. It is called the Age of Intuition.

Now, each month represents a given time when the earth is passing one of the twelve solar systems. Thus, we say April represents ARIES, etc. Now, our Sun, as the center of attraction, is continually in sympathetic vibration with all the other suns and planets within a radius of its attractive power. So, as our earth passes between our sun and a Solar

System, it receives the full force of this magnetic current. Hence, a child born at a time when the Earth was passing between Gemini and the Sun. time, May 20 to June 21, would be marked with the character of a Gemini. This child would begin its embryotic growth during the month of September, under the Sign Virgo. Now, every three months the earth will pass one of Gemini's poles and will be marked with some of the characteristics of the Signs Virgo, Sagittarius and Pisces; as the first, third and sixth months are the most impressionable period of the young embryo's growth. Hence, you will see why it is every Gemini will show some of the traits of character of the above named signs. This example will suffice to explain all others.

CHAPTER III.

The Elements, Systems and Temperaments of the Grand Man.

There are four fundamental elements in the construction of worlds. They are Fire, Earth, Air and Water. These elements are also the bases of all growth and changes in the phenomena of life. Now divide our Zodiac by four, and we find a group of three signs ruled by each of these elements, as follows:

Signs	Element	Systems.	Temperaments.
ARIES, LEO, SAGITTARIUS	Fire	Blood	Vital.
TAURUS, VIRGO, CAPRICORN	Earth	Bones and Muscles	Motive.
GEMINI, LIBRA, AQUARIUS	Air	Nerves	Mental.
CANCER, SCORPIO, PISCES	Water	Digestive Organs	Lymphatic.

In the human body we find four systems, as follows: Bones, Muscles, Blood and Nerves.

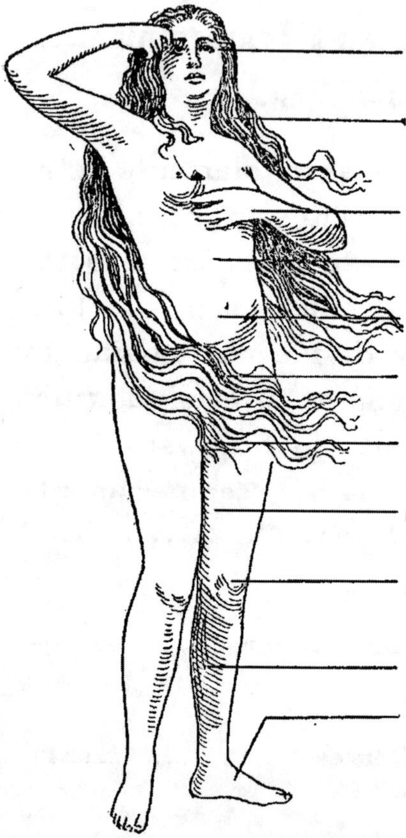

♈ Aries.	Fire.	Mch. 21 to Apr. 19.
♉ Taurus.	Earth.	Apr. 19 to May 20.
♊ Gemini.	Air.	May 20 to June 21.
♋ Cancer.	Water.	June 21 to July 22.
♌ Leo.	Fire.	July 22 to Aug. 22.
♍ Virgo.	Earth.	Aug. 22 to Sept. 23.
♎ Libra.	Air.	Sept. 23 to Oct. 23.
♏ Scorpio.	Water.	Oct. 23 to Nov. 22.
♐ Sagittarius.	Fire.	Nov. 22 to Dec. 21.
♑ Capricorn.	Earth.	Dec. 21 to Jan. 20.
♒ Aquarius.	Air.	Jan. 20 to Feb. 19.
♓ Pisces.	Water.	Feb. 19 to Mch. 21.

PLATE No. 2.

and Digestive Organs. Now they are ruled in their development by the elements which precede them in above table,

Carrying this still further we find under the head of Phrenology, four temperaments, as follows: Vital, Motive, Mental, Lymphatic. Each temperament is ruled by a certain element. See table. Thus, we find the magnetic rays from the Signs of the Zodiac are responsible for the many peculiar temperaments shown in life. It acts upon all life, animal and vegetable; even the mineral world is controlled by these mighty forces. We also notice that each sign has its corresponding pole in the human body, as you will see in engraving No. 2. Thus, Aries, the first sign in the mental trinity, represents the head of the Grand Man, and should be celebrated as the beginning of the year.

The folly of following an old, senseless custom, celebrating the new year, as we do, the beginning of January, is out of harmony with all natural law. On the 21st of March the sun crosses the spring equinox, proclaiming, "Spring is here!" All nature puts on her gayest attire and celebrates the event, except stupid man, the only creatnre held back from obeying natural instincts by his own foolish customs and prejudices.

In giving the Characteristics of the twelve Signs of the Zodiac, I shall follow my own observation, and shall tell you what I have observed or discovered, independent of what others have said; as I believe each one has a right to an opinion. I claim mine.

CHAPTER IV.

♈

Aries.

HEAD SIGN OF THE FIRE TRIPLICITY.

March 21 to April 19.

This sign rules the head of the Grand Man. As a rule, people born in this sign have considerable executive ability, and sometimes make fine scholars.

I have found many types of people in this sign; a few small people, but, as a rule, there are three types—the large, fair complexion Aries, and the smaller, dark complexion Aries. The former are more inclined to education and have a calm. gentle disposition, and are not inclined to any great amount of exertion. They do make splendid teachers owing to their fine patience and self-control. They also possess literary ability. The latter type are more executive, quick in movement, determined to carry through whatever they undertake, and will grieve and worry if thwarted in their plans. The one other class of people born in this sign are a mixture between the other two. A large dark one will possess the elements of both energy and patience, and are the strongest people born in this sign. The one fine trait of character in these people is their quick response to duty. They make splendid husbands and wives; are fine providers and sacrifice a great deal for those they love. The diseases of Aries are usually brain or nervous troubles. They should avoid inharmony and learn to take frequent rests. They should also beware of stomach troubles and paralysis. The Aries child should never be treated harshly. Parents will find better results through kindness and patience, than they will by using force on these childern.

Some of our greatest generals and statesmen were born in this sign. Jefferson, Buchanan, Henry Clay, Bismarck. Edward Bellamy are among the prominent Aries. Children born in this sign should have a splendid education. The congenial companions for Aries people should be chosen from Gemini, Libra, Sagittarius, Capricorn.

CHAPTER V.

♉

Taurus.

HEAD SIGN OF THE EARTH TRIPLICITY.

April 19 to May 20.

This sign rules the neck and the cerebellum brain, which is the seat of muscular motion in the body. These people are usually fair complexion, slow and deliberate in motion, very exact and careful in what they do. They are, therefore, adapted to scientific work. They become inventors and discoverers in the mental as well as mechanical work. They are noted for their great classifying ability. They are fearless in expressing an opinion, and are not easily backed down in an argument. They have fine intuition and are quite inspirational, yet they become better writers than speakers. They are grand friends and sometimes bitter enemies. Their capacity for money making is small, and what they do have is usually spent freely for others. They are a very unselfish, sympathetic people. Their one great fault is their temper, which is quick and boisterous. You will usually know when a Taurus is angry, as the storm is terrific while it lasts, but they easily quiet down and will forgive quickly.

I have met a few fine singers in this sign, but they have to be careful of their throats, as that is their weak point; are also subject, as all motive people are, to rheumatism. A child in this sign, or any other for that matter, should not be plagued or irritated as it will tend to spoil their temper and ruin their digestive system; as their anger is so intense it will leave its effects for days in the system. Yet those dear little Taurus children are often plagued nearly to death by older children, simply because they are quick tempered. The Taurus people have great memory; they will find their best friends in Capricorn, Libra and sometimes Pisces. Dr. Sivartha, one of the greatest living scientists, Shakespeare, novelist, Preston, historian, are a few of the thinkers born in Taurus. This sign rules the faculties of science in the brain. Their diseases are heart troubles, tumors and peculiar blood diseases.

CHAPTER VI.

♊

Gemini.

HEAD SIGN OF THE AIR TRIPLICITY.

May 20 to June 21.

This sign rules the hands, arms and lungs of the Grand Man. They are as a rule very executive and very versatile, and as they can turn their hands to any kind of work, they are liable to become Jacks of all trades and masters of none. They invariably lack in stability and continuity, and, as they possess a restless disposition, they will try a half-dozen occupations before they settle, which is a doubtful proposition if they ever do. I have found Geminis do not amount to much until they become conscious of their inner life and seek to unfold their wonderful spiritual nature. Then their intuition and inspiration is grand. Just as versatile in thought as in action, they make brilliant public speakers. They are the people who change their minds readily; a new truth today becomes old tomorrow. They have been well styled continual seekers after wisdom and culture. On the lower plane of mental development, where they have not yet discovered their spiritual nature, you will find them extremely conservative, timid, melancholy, afraid to trust their own opinions, suspicious of friends, and have a great love of wealth, but as they recognize their higher selves, they change, their natures become possessed with a wonderful degree of self-confidence, and they will boldly proclaim the new truths with a total disregard as to the opinions of others.

R. W. Emerson, Benjamin Fay Mills, Margaret Fuller Orsoly, Walter Whitman, Harriet Beecher Stowe were born in this sign and are fine representatives of Gemini genius, Queen Victoria was also born under this sign. Her reign is considered a remarkable one in many ways, but it is evident she never became fully conscious of her inner nature, or she would have established many mighty reforms for the good of her people, and would have scattered her £40,000,000 among her starving nations before she died, for a more generous, kind hearted, courageous people than the awakened Gemini are not born.

The diseases from which they suffer are nervous diseases and stomach trouble, brought on, as a rule, by overwork, also nervous prostration and sometimes lung troubles. Their remedy is rest and harmony. Kind friends who understand them are better than medicine.

Their best friends are found in Aquarius, Aries, Virgo, Pisces Gemini and Libra.

CHAPTER VII.

♋

Cancer.

HEAD SIGN OF THE WATER TRIPLICITY.

June 21 to July 22.

This sign rules the breast of the Grand Man. All the water people are sensitive people, and Cancer is no exception to the rule,—more sensitive, if anything. They are, when not too fleshy, large, splendid looking people; they have commanding figures, large heads, strong features. They are a very determined people, and have considerable tact in dealing with the masses; they have splendid intellects and a love of reform; and often become great organizers. Eleanor Kirk says they are as strong as giants or as weak as infants, which is quite true. You will find them bravely carrying great burdens, and, at the same time, fretting over some trifling thing. They are usually afraid of poverty, and are sometimes penurious and stingy, but I do not know of anyone who will take a little and make so much out of it as a Cancer, when they have to. They are fond of the beautiful and artistic and will always manage to dress well; you will find them sometimes displaying a great amount of jewelry; they are the men who will wear their watch chains spread across their vests, will wear large diamonds; the women will pin their watches and other jewelry where they can be seen. There are those besides Cancers who will show this foolish love of display, but it is more pronounced in their nature. These people are neat and orderly, and the women are fine housekeepers, as a rule. Every Cancer child should be well educated; like the Gemini, they improve rapidly when given an opportunity; they readily take to the occult studies and become beautiful teachers along these lines. The Cancer woman has a great deal of trouble in marriage. I have known them to have as high as three divorces before thirty-seven; they should never marry young, unless fully conscious of what they are about, and should carefully select their mates. I have found more divorces in this sign than nearly all the others put together; the cause is, we think, they have such an artistic, ideal nature, it is seldom they can realize in the opposite sex that ideal, and they are liable to tire quickly of the routine duties of an inharmonious life.

They will find their most congenial friends in Pisces or Scorpio, Libra or Aquarius.

The diseases are poor digestion, dropsy, cancers, tumors and blood diseases.

Henry Ward Beecher, Richard Henry Stoddard and Nathaniel Hawthorne were born in this sign.

CHAPTER VIII.

♌

Leo.

MIDDLE SIGN OF THE FIRE TRIPLICITY.

July 22 to August 22.

This sign rules the heart of the Grand Man. The Leo people represent very well the symbol of their sign, for a more couragious, fearless, magnetic people does not live. They are supposed to carry the palm for physical beauty, and I have found the statement to be quite true; but they do not seem to be conscious of the fact; if so, it does not spoil them. They are natural leaders, and when sufficiently intelligent to lead, make successful ones. When undeveloped, they are domineering, headstrong and truly vicious in their attacks on those who oppose them. They are supposed to possess the finest attributes for public speakers. I have known a few in this sign. Alfred Tennyson, Robert Ingersoll, Rev. Moody and David Crockett were born in this sign. They represent the religious faculties in the brain, and you will find them either stoutly defending religion or tearing it down. They possess a fine sense of taste, and, for that reason, are supposed to make fine cooks. I have found a great many, both men and women, who are good cooks, but, as a rule, they do not like to work with their hands; they make better planners than executors.

They are true friends and bitter enemies. Never let a Leo know you are afraid of him; if you do, you might as well move out; they are great bluffers; they usually make their way easily through life, and seldom meet with misfortune. This sign is ruled by the sun, causing them to be quick tempered, passionate people and not always true to their mates. They are of medium build, usually with dark eyes and hair and fair skin.

Their finest companions will be found in Gemini, Libra or Aquarius.

The diseases are weak heart action and indigestion.

CHAPTER IX.

♍

Virgo.

MIDDLE SIGN OF THE EARTH TRIPLICITY.

August 22 to September 23.

This sign rules the Solar Plexus in the Grand Man. The Solar Plexus is the intuitive brain of the body, that brain which never sleeps, always active and watchful for the best interests of the body. It is to the body what the mother is to the home, dependent as is also the mother upon the positive brain for support at the same time, the real support of the positive or head brain. Its function is to rule all the organic life force in the body and when this brain is recognized and obeyed great health and harmony will be the result, not only in the individual, but in society also, which is but a duplicate of the individual.

People born in this sign represent to humanity, intuition, motherhood, unselfish love and a strong protective interest in all whom their lives come in contact with. This is the musical sign of the Zodiac. It also gives us some grand mediums. As a rule, they are pure, soul inspiring people; yet they are often misunderstood, and sometimes have bitter enemies; they make enemies by the too free use of criticism. The mass of the people are yet too ignorant to stand blunt criticism, and the undeveloped Virgo usually paints his ideas in no mild tints; black is black, and he will not hesitate to tell you so. As he develops his spiritual nature, he will tone down the rougher shades and become a beautiful companion and friend. They are sometimes quite successful in business. They have strong, large bodies, and are considered the most healthy people in the world. Usually the complexion is fair.

They find their best friends in Gemini, Aries, Aquarius or Capricorn.

Oliver Wendell Holmes, Frances Willard and Robert Burdette were born in this sign.

CHAPTER X.

♎

Libra.

MIDDLE SIGN OF AIR TRIPLICITY.

September 23 to October 23.

This sign rules the loins and kidneys of the Grand Man, also the faculties in the brain of rulership and ambition. While this sign is supposed to be the more highly endowed with inspiration and psychic force, my experience is but a few become conscious of the fact and make any use of these beautiful qualities; they are usually timid and afraid to trust to their own judgment. I have found them, as a rule careless in money matters; that is,so far as making it is concerned, but have not found them dishonest. They are people who have very few enemies, as they are not quick to take sides.

They have fine intellects, strong intuition and could make splendid writers or speakers, if they would develop more self-confidence, which they usually lack; they have large hope, and are not easily discouraged. A few successful business men are in this sign, but, as a rule, they are too careless with money to succeed to any great extent.

They are easily imposed upon and will take advice from others too readily for their own good. They are a restless, moving people, fond of excitement and change, extremely sensitive; they cannot stand to be scolded or found fault with; usually quick tempered, and when angry, have a way of saying things which hurt deeply. The best results with a Libra child are gained through praise, and the child should, as soon as possible, be put upon its own merits, encouraged and stimulated, never discouraged. In this way, one can strengthen and assist the Libra to use his beautiful gift of inspiration. They are a kind loving, gentle people, and under a more proper system of education, when all this truth is more fully understood by parents and teachers, the Libra sign may yet develop wonderful people.

A few under the present system have developed prominence as rulers. We find four Presidents were born in this sign: John Adams, Gen. Arthur, R. B. Hayes and Z. Taylor.

This sign should never mate with Pisces or Virgo. Pisces always wants a reason, and Libra cannot explain; and Virgo's criticism would drive Libra mad.

Their most congenial companions are born in Aquarius, Taurus or Capricorn, sometimes Gemini, if both are in the same plane of development. This is true of all signs. One should mate with an equal mentally and physically, and then seek to keep up with one another.

The diseases of Libra are similar to Gemini; nervous prostration, peculiar stomach trouble and pains across the back, caused by weakness of the kidneys, which Libra is sure to show during some portion of his life.

CHAPTER XI.

♏

Scorpio.

MIDDLE SIGN OF WATER TRIPLICITY.

October 23 to November 23.

This sign governs the genital organs, the groins, bladder and sex functions of the Grand Man.

There are two classes of people born in this sign, and great attention should be paid on the part of parents as to which class their child represents. If it shows a well balanced brain and hand, you have nothing to fear, as the well organized Scorpio is as strong and reliable as any people in the world; they make splendid managers, kind and proficient parents and teachers, faithful as friends, or in any position ot trust. As a rule, they do better when working for others, but I have known them to be very successful in their own business. This sign rules the faculties of industry in the brain; therefore, the well developed

Scorpios will be industrious, persevering, patient in details, and will work for others' interests equally as well as for their own; but an undeveloped, poorly organized Scorpio is one to be feared. He is never weak, but is, many times, vicious. If he starts down the ladder of life, he is quite sure to go to the bottom.

I have known some very low, depraved people in this sign, and some very grand characters. Great care should be taken to teach these children in regard to the uses and abuses of the sex nature, and to overcome their selfish, jealous passions, which are sometimes very strong.

James A. Garfield, Elizabeth Cady Stanton and William Cullen Bryant were born in this sign.

The diseases of Scorpio are weakness in back and sex organs, lumbago and gout.

They find their congenial companions in Taurus, Virgo or Pisces.

CHAPTER XII.

♐

Sagittarius.

NEGATIVE POLE OF FIRE TRIPLICITY.

November 23 to December 21.

This sign governs the hips and thighs of the Grand Man.

People born in this sign are noted for their great stability and determination to carry through whatever they undertake; they are fearless aud brave, and are always noted for minding their own business. One thing at a time is all a Sagittarius can attend to, and he will become nervous and disturbed when called upon to perform a half-dozen duties at the same time. In this respect they are very much unlike their Solar mate, Gemini, who delights in having a number of irons in the fire; they do not like to give up beaten in any enterprise, and will hold on with bulldog tenacity until sometimes they will lose every dollar they have, health thrown in. They should learn that the man who fights and runs away may live to fight another day; in other words, they should learn to sometimes let go, as we can carry all things to extremes, and also that sometimes it is impossible to have one's own way. They are usually afraid of public opinion and dread being called a failure; they are very sensitive and many of them possess fine mediumistic talents. This sign rules the faculties of wealth in the brain, and while these people are not miserly or stingy, yet they pin a great deal of faith in money, and you will usually find them well supplied. As their talents are varied, they can turn their hands to many kinds of work; they are naturally industrious and saving, and are sure to accumulate. They are kind, loving friends, and you will always find them ready and willing to help you under any emergency. Some of the grandest people in the world are in this, in many ways, the finest sign of the Zodiac.

Wendell Phillips, Mary E. Livermore and John Milton were born in this sign. Mary E. Livermore's life is a splendid example of the kindness and tenacity of this sign.

The diseases of Sagittarius people are rheumatism, stomach trouble and nervousness.

They will find their congenial companions in Aries, Gemini, Virgo or Libra.

CHAPTER XIII.

♑

Capricorn.

NEGATIVE SIGN OF EARTH TRIPLICITY.

December 21 to January 20.

This sign rules the knees of the Grand Man. Its symbol is the goat, and the people born within its limits represent it well. They are a restless, turbulent people, always on the move, and, like the goat, will pick their living where others will starve. This sign rules the faculties of commerce in the brain, and among the males, we often find great speculators and financiers; they excel as money makers, and are very materialistic in all their ideas; they do not like to work for others, and consequently, do their best when working for themselves. The great builders, civil engineers and explorers are found in this sign. The females often become fine teachers and beautiful mothers, as they are naturally fond of plants, animals or children. When the Capricorn becomes conscious of, and develops, his spiritual nature, his usefulness to society cannot be limited. He is peace loving and slow to anger, but when aroused he has a fearful temper while it lasts, but he recovers himself quickly and forgives easily. He likes to dress well, is a good entertainer and a great talker.

The ruling planet of this sign is Saturn, which develops a deep love of nature. You will find them all fond of plants and animals, also many fine artists will be found in this sign. These children should always have a good business education and early in life be put on their own responsibility. Once get a Capricorn child to promise obedience and you have gained a point, as they are, as a rule, very truthful; these children will love to run away when quite small and explore the neighborhood, but they will generally return all right; they have large faculties of location, and can always find their way home.

Stonewall Jackson and Cicero were born in this sign.

Their diseases are rheumatism in the joints,

especially the knees, and sometimes indigestion, which is usually caused by eating too fast, as the Capricorn is always in a hurry. When ill, they should seek a quiet rural district, as nature will more quickly restore them to health than doctors or medicine.

Their congenial friends are Taurus, Virgo, Libra and Aries.

CHAPTER XIV.

♒

Aquarius.

NEGATIVE SIGN OF AIR TRIPLICITY.

January 20 to February 19.

This sign rules the ankles of the Grand Man. It is the home of those who are quiet, patient and faithful in their mental and moral ways. This sign rules the faculties of home in the brain; therefore, these people are fond of home, great lovers of fair play and justice and equity. It is said they are the strongest and the weakest people in the world, and I believe it is true; but they are never vicious. When weak, they will go to the extreme in physical and moral degradation, but, unlike Scorpio, they will seldom injure another. Parents should at once note the thumbs of their young Aquarius children—a small, weak thumb will tell the story; the thumb represents the will, and if it is too small, the child will be easily led. Parents should use every means to encourage and develop their will, for the lack of will in a child causes them to be careless, forgetful inattentive in school and disobedient to parents; they will desire to obey, but as soon as they meet other children, they forget what has been told them; they are tossed about by every wind that blows. This is true of every child who is the possessor of small, weak thumbs.

But when the Aquarius is strong, he is very strong, without doubt, the strongest mentally and morally of all the signs in the Zodiac. This sign represents the breath of life, therefore these people are as necessary to society as air is to the lungs of the Grand Man; they are a peace loving people, yet, if danger menaces the home, they will fight until they conquer or are killed. Some of the greatest and most dearly beloved people in the world's history were born in this sign. Abraham Lincoln, James G. Blaine, Susan B. Anthony, Edgar Allen Poe, William Jennings Bryan, Henry W. Longfellow, Samuel J. Tilden and President McKinley are a few of the prominent people of this sign.

Sometimes these people take to the trades,

but are seldom successful in mechanical lines; they do better in the professions. Every Aquarius child should have a splendid education; they are fond of study, and, as they are possessed of a good memory and keen perception, they make rapid progress; they should not be allowed to associate with coarse, low companions, as they will as readily absorb immoral as moral teaching—and, remember in all cases, as the twig is bent the tree will grow; they are fond of nature and make fine artists and musicians. This sign has less trouble in marriage than any other; they have a faculty of getting along with almost everybody.

Their congenial signs are Gemini, Libra, Virgo and sometimes Leo. When these people are ruled by the moon, it produces a restless disposition, and they travel a great deal.

Their diseases are weakness of the chest and lungs and nervous troubles.

CHAPTER XV.

Pisces.

♓

NEGATIVE POLE OF WATER TRIPLICITY.

February 19 to March 21.

This sign rules the feet of the Grand Man. The people born in this sign are, in some respects, the most peculiar and difficult to understand of all the twelve signs. They are loving and kind hearted, always ready to assist in time of trouble, and always trying to help others to the front, but are backward in using their own talents, which, in many instances, are very strong. They are usually gifted along the lines of art, becoming fine designers and artists; the females excel as designers in millinery and dressmaking, or in any department of artistic work; the males are proficient as bookkeepers, accountants and telegraph operators; they also make quite a success as physicians.

The Pisces are willing servers, if one takes

the right way with them; they are exceedingly sensitive, and cannot stand to be scolded or found fault with; they, to do their best, should have their own way, as far as possible, in all things. Many a Pisces child has been spoiled in early life by not being understood by parents or guardians. One should never order a Pisces child to do anything; they are willing cooperators, but they cannot be driven; the driving process only tends to develop a stubborn, vicious nature; it develops the faculties of combativeness and destructiveness so large that, in many instances, it spoils their after life. They have a great faculty for asking questions which will lead to an argument; but I have found it is folly to argue with the average Pisces, as they will, nine times out of ten, dispute you, even when they know they are wrong, just to be contrary. As a rule, they talk too much. Once they learn the value of silence and self control, and become liberal enough to see their own faults, and correct them, they are the most useful and valuable members of society.

The diseases that Pisces people are subject to are pains in the head, feet and back, and weakness in the digestive organs.

Their best friends are in Virgo, Cancer and Scorpio. They do not mate well with the air or fire people.

George Washington, Pope Leo, Andrew Jackson and James Madison found their birthplace in Pisces. When the Pisces has a proper early training, and learn to use their spiritual senses, the work they can accomplish for good of humanity is not easily outdone by any other people.

CHAPTER XVI.

Why Should We Learn the Signs of the Zodiac?

The student who wishes to become proficient in Palmistry should first learn thoroughly the Signs of the Zodiac, so he can call up the character instantly to his mind of each of the signs. The reason for this is, many times you will meet with people who are having trouble with a friend, husband or wife. Now, if you know the sign each was born in, you can understand the case instantly, and be able to give better advice. Remember there are always two sides to every story. I have often had people come to me with a tale of woe in regard to another, and by a little careful inquiry, have found the trouble was caused by misunderstanding one another, and a few words is often enough to convince your visitor that such is the case. I am positive, in my own mind, divorces could be avoided nine times out of ten, if people would study one another more carefully, and especially study one's self, as *we* may be the one to blame. Let us search carefully for the weeds of error in our own natures, and once having discovered them, never rest until they are destroyed, root and branch. There is none so blind as he who will not see. Let us be not of that number. One should also learn the different triplicities, so that you may be able to explain the relations one sign bears to another.

CHAPTER XVII.

The Planets.

The next in order is the Planets. You can study their size, time and orbits from the chart, but I will give some of the qualities developed by each. In the chart, you will observe, each planet is in its own sign, or home, as it is sometimes called. Thus, Saturn is at home in Capricorn, and exercises its strongest influence upon life when in that sign; the same of all the others. Planetary influence has a tendency to increase or diminish the character of a sign to a certain degree, but rarely do they change the character so much that you cannot tell the ruling sign, or, in other words, the sign they were born in. Under the head of Palmistry, we explain fully how this is accomplished. One must refer to an Ephemeris to find the position of each planet at birth.

PLANETS AND THEIR SIGNS.

☿,

Mercury, the smallest planet, whose orbit is nearest the sun, is called the God of Finance and Science.

♀,

The second planet, Venus, the God of Love.

☾

The Moon, the God of Romance and Travel.

♂,

Mars, the God of War.

♃,

Jupiter, the God of Intellect and Ambition. This planet gives brain illumination.

♄,

Saturn, the God of Nature.

♅,

Uranus is a neutral planet. He acts always

with the strongest in power. If the strongest is good, he is good, and vice versa.

☉

The Sun is the God of Physical Success, Glory and Fame.

♆.

Neptune is the God of the Spiritual.

Now, the magnetic influence of these planets develops certain faculties in the brain, and those faculties again polarize in the hand, as we shall see later, under the head of the Mounts of the Hand. In Palmistry, we will take up the study of the planets more thoroughly. My object in this chapter is to simply point out to you a few fundamental principles, that you may better understand the beautiful Science of Palmistry, which will be the final work in the book. In the Science of Palmistry, we find a blending of all the other sciences that are used for the purpose of character reading.

CHAPTER XVIII.

The Two Brain Centers in Man.

Now let us turn our attention for a time to the Head Brain of man, that piece of mechanism which has been so little studied or understood, as yet, by the masses. The brain is the great dynamo of the body, with its millions of nerve cells, divided into its numerous groups of faculties, ruled so perfectly by its two centers, which correspond with the positive and negative forces in all nature. Let us turn for a moment to the chart of the Zodiac. You will see two suns in the ellipse. In all modern works on Astronomy, they now recognize our Solar System to be an ellipse. *We* know we are nearer the sun at certain times of the year by our own observation. Now, if our Sun is in one pole of the ellipse, what balances in the other pole? We claim, by all the laws of nature and science, there is another sun there, which acts in the Solar System as the Solar

Plexus does in the human body, or the feminine center in the brain.

The sun we see with our physical eyes is the positive, or male sun. In the opposite pole we have the negative, or female sun, unknown to us because we have not yet developed our spiritual sense of sight.

I recognize a duality of senses in the human body—five physical senses and five spiritual. All our education in the past has been of such a character as to develop our physical senses, and to consider them all-sufficient; but our modern *research* along metaphysical lines reveals the spiritual senses and the need of developing them in this life. We develop them, and, lo! a new heaven and a new earth appear; life takes on a greater and grander meaning; the mother God in nature appears in all her glory, and we behold the wonderful plan of life, which no longer seems incomplete and out of harmony, but that all things work together for the glory of God, or good, toward building up a perfect universe.

But let us return to the Zodiac again. Having recognized the two suns, let us note their influence upon our earth. You will see the spiritual sun is on the right, and the physical sun on the left, of the Zodiac. Now, how is it, when our earth is nearer the male sun we have winter, and nearer the female sun we have summer? Yes, I know the theory of the astronomers. but I have a right to mine. and it is this:—as the female is the developing element in all nature, so does the female sun hold the developing power; the male sun is as the male or positive force in all nature, the projector, the sustaining and protecting element in the household of the Solar System; the united force of these two suns create, build and sustain the planetary system, of which our earth is a child. The other great Solar Systems, known as the Signs of the Zodiac, are neighbors, and they and their children make up the society of the Solar Heavens. The more remote a neighbor, the less his influence has to do with our lives. Now, in studying Astrology in this manner, we see it in a practical light which robs it of all its mystical power.

CHAPTER XIX.

The Duality of Forces.

Now, having recognized the positive and negative centers in the Solar System, let us take the microcosm man, and there again we discover this duality of forces. I have referred before to the two brain or nerve centers in the human body, under the sign Virgo, but I wish to bring it out more clearly, for in men and women scientifically understanding this point hinges the readjustment of society on the plan of justice and equity. As we see, each sun in the Solar System possesses both positive and negative qualities; for part of the time the physical sun is attracting, and part of the time repelling, and the spiritual sun the same. Yet, the developing attributes are stronger in the female sun, and the positive or protective attributes are stronger in the male sun. We note the same principle, or condition throughout all animal life.

The two brains in the body are called male and female; the Solar Plexus is the female brain and the brain in the head is male. Every human being has both brain centers, but in woman the solar brain predominates and in man the head brain. One represents intuition, the other, reason.

Let us take up these two centers and see what service they render the human organism. The Solar Plexus is that large nerve center just back of the stomach. Its mission is to regulate and control the organic structure of the body. This brain never sleeps, or ceases to perform its work through life. When all the physical senses are clothed in slumber, the spiritual senses, which have their being in the Solar Plexus brain, go right on with their never ceasing work; the heart beats, sending the blood to all parts of the body, building up here, tearing down there; the lungs continue carrying the oxygen required by the blood, and carrying out the poisonous gases (oh, how necessary it is we have large, well aired bed chambers); the digestive organs continue their labor. All this goes on without the slightest assistance from the male brain, but, after a time, the material in the digestive organs, which goes to build up the blood and body as a whole, becomes exhausted, then a call is sent to the positive brain for more material, and, one by one, the male faculties, or physical senses, awaken and become conscious a call has been made on them for something; the spiritual brick builders are out of material, and the hod carriers must get to work.

Now, we see in the human brain two centers; one is called motus, the other, sensus; one controls motion, the other, sensation. Here, again, one is male, the other, female—positive and negative; the female center is first to respond to the Solar Plexus brain for food. Along the nerves of sensation to the feminine center in the brain flashes the message, and we become conscious we are hungry. Now the message is passed on to the positive, or motus, center, to move the muscles, and get something to eat; and for its own self protection, it must obey; but the Solar Plexus sends another message, and that is for a certain kind of food. She, in her cell building, requires certain kinds of material, just as the brick builder requires so many brick and so much mortar; but suppose the hod carriers take back all brick or all mortar, or a little green cheese, just to please his fancy, instead of either brick or mortar, what kind of a house do you suppose the brick builder would construct? Just the same kind of structure as we build when we disobey in eating, when we let the physical sense of taste rule, eat to gratify our passions, regardless whether the builder can use what we send her. Is it any wonder we grow frail and weak? As a race, we are growing smaller and less healthy each generation. Look at the condition of our teeth, and our bones, muscles and nerves are no better. Nearly everything we eat is adulterated, and what we drink is no better. Imagine sending down into the stomach such poisons as thene, caffeine, nicotine, alcohol and a hundred other poisons which we are continually administering to the body, in the form of drugs and impure air.

Then there is another side, the side of poverty, where the Solar Plexus calls in vain for nourishment, and the head brain is powerless to respond, only with an insufficient amount of fourth class material. The result of all this is weakness and decay to the whole human organism.

In human society,—which is again the exact duplicate of the inner man, made up of two elements, positive and negative, male and female; as with the microcosm man, so with the macrocosm society—the male has assumed control, not only of himself, but of the female also. Now, she is to the body politic what the Solar Plexus is to the human body, or the spiritual sun to the Solar System; but are her wishes regarded, her commands obeyed? No. She is told she is a fool, more or less, and her mission is to obey. Obey what? Why, the male. The male? that positive force whose work in all nature consists only in carrying out and protecting the wishes of its greater life? Look at our man made society today, and we have a beautiful example of disobedience along the above named lines. Everywhere there is strife and contention; the social digestive organs are badly out of order. Its blood is poisoned, great sores raise on its body, in the form of wars, prostitution, intemperance and murder; it is covered with the pimples of greed, selfishness, theft and discontent. We have already tried every means that brain can conceive to deal with this effect. We have burned and scourged these sores; we have applied all sorts of salves, and now, after all these centuries, we make the discovery we have been dealing only with the effect of a great cause, whose roots reach to the very vitals of human life and society. We must first learn that this is an orderly universe, and that it is governed by great laws, which we cannot disobey without receiving the penalty of disobedience. Under this great universal law of cause and effect, woman has her place and man his also. Now, the man cannot occupy the woman's place any more than electricity can do the work of magnetism, or vice versa. Each have their proper place, and when they occupy it, great harmony to the home and society will be the result.

Harmony is life, inharmony is death; which do we prefer?

Now, I do not want my readers to think I take a partial view of this question because I am a woman. I am also a mother, and my only child is a son; and surely I have as much interest in his life as I have in my own; but I have arrived in thought and desire at the plane of universal motherhood, and I claim by the right of motherhood, all children are mine, boys and girls alike. I love them all, and would see them well and happy, which is their natural right. So, dear reader, as you follow out my conclusions, try to lay aside sex for a time, and let us seek to break the barriers which hold apart the race, and rejoice in the at-one-ment of all life, as we journey back to our Creator; for our interest, male and female, is identical, after all.

What place in human society should woman fill?—the knotty question of the age, I say, by all the laws of science and nature, she should occupy the position of dictator, adviser, teacher and counsellor. The spiritual senses are more highly developed in woman than in man; her intuition is keener; she has a natural foresight which the male does not possess, at least, to the same degree. How many times have we heard the man say, "If I had only listened to my wife, how much better it would have been for me." The man's education has been always to the detriment of woman; trained only to regard his physical senses, and to be ashamed to show any emotion, which is the female element in him, is it any wonder he looks upon woman as something to be excused, and usually to be ashamed of? Did you ever hear a little boy say, Oh, she is only a 'sissy' !" and notice the contempt he will throw into his voice? Now, if he had been trained to recognize his spiritual senses, to listen to the still, small voice, as it is sometimes called, he would see the little girl was the embodiment of his highest and holiest life.

Again, man regards woman as a slave, more or less. Her great work has been a hidden work, even as the work of our inner organic mother. Yet, what a work it has been ! The mother of nations, she has toiled on against tremendous odds. Oh, man ! her cause beats beneath your own heart, and, as you listen to its measured beats, and feel the warm blood flow through your veins, and experience the sensations of pleasure and sorrow, remember it all comes from the female elements within you. Note your fine intuitions, your gradual development of brotherhood, and your growing dislike of brutality; these are attributes of the female. It is the mother speaking in her son, and when she tells you, "My boy, send me pure food, that I may build you a strong body," you cannot afford to disobey; and when she tells you to love, cherish and protect the beautiful companion of your life, in which she is more fully represented, again, obey. Make conditions for that young life, of which you are the direct cause; for how can the young mother do her best, and produce a perfect child, unless she again be obeyed? Her maternal instincts tell her what she requires in this marvelous building, and if it be not forthcoming, a defective life is the result. Like the Solar Plexus, whom can she depend on to carry out her desires but you, and what are the conditions she requires in this work? First, a full and untrammelled liberty; second, that she come not, during her *life*, in contact with vice, crime or disease, for just as long as she does, she will transmit the same to her offspring; third, that she secure from you a willing cooperation in the carrying out of all her plans or desires for her and your good.

Now, the woman also possesses the male

attributes, and after so long trying to get a hearing from her own plane, and being continually turned down, and seeing her handiwork slowly destroyed, she at last begins to turn. She is now developing her male attributes, like the animal, in order to protect herself, and, in some instances, they are predominating, as in the case of Mrs. Nation. Yet, who can blame her? Motherhood everywhere defied and defiled, in male and female alike, is it any wonder the worm at last turns, and tries to protect its own?

But we must leave this field of thought, realizing we have only thrown out a few grains; but who can estimate the value of a few grains, when sown in the right soil?

CHAPTER XX.

The Head and Its Relation to the Hand.

According to the science of Phrenology, we find thirty-six faculties in the human brain, (some Phrenologists claim forty-two); which we divide as follows (Note engraving No. 3): From center of ears across the forehead, from eye to top of forehead, we have twelve faculties; these we call the Intellectual faculties; from center of ears over top of head, from forehead to crown, twelve more. these we call the emotional faculties; from center of ears across back head, from crown to base of brain, twelve others; this group represents the will, or expression. The hand has also three parts. and it polarizes with the brain as follows: the nerves descending from the intellectual faculties polarize in the fingers; twelve phalanges, twelve faculties. The emotional faculties polarize in the palm, and the faculties of the will polarize in the thumb. The stu-

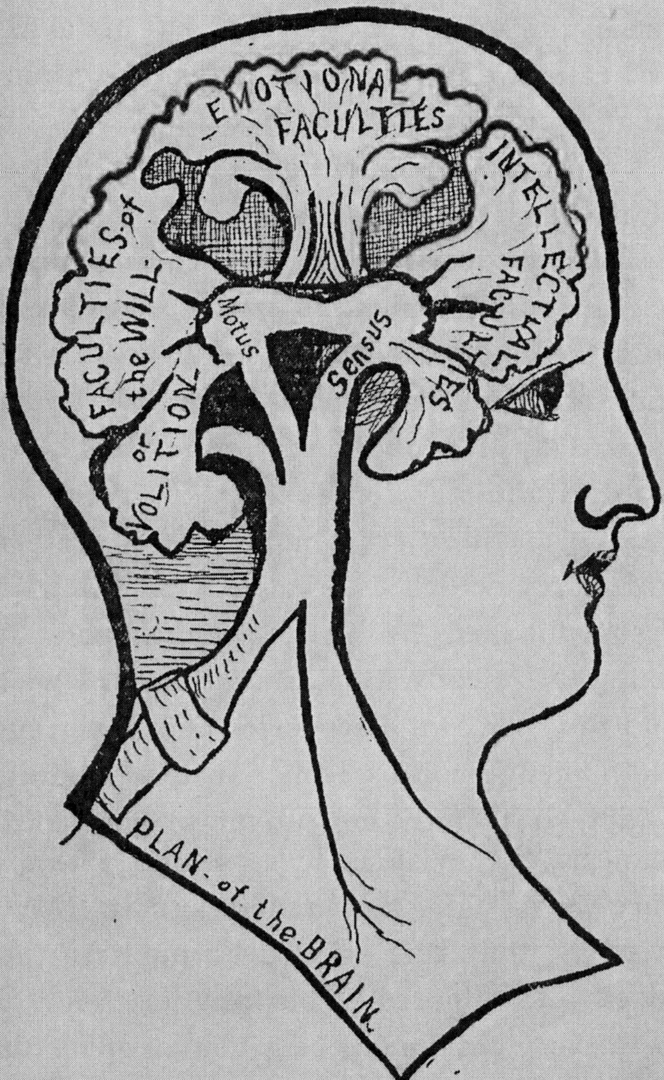
EMOTIONAL FACULTIES
INTELLECTUAL FACULTIES
FACULTIES of the WILL
VOLITION
Motus
Sensus
PLAN of the BRAIN

PLATE No. 3.

dent can at once see the beautiful relation between the brain and the hand. This is as far as I take up Phrenology, as I find Palmistry much more reliable in all its details.

I want my reader to note here the necessity of reading the whole hand; so many think Palmistry consists in merely reading the lines in the palm, which, as you see, represents only the emotional nature. The palm, to be sure, is a very interesting part of Palmistry, as will appear under its proper head. The word Palmistry is derived from the word Palma, meaning, the hand. This system of Palmistry which I practice and teach, was first published by Dr. Sivartha, and, after four years steady work, in this field, I wish to add to it my own discoveries and experiences, and I pledge you I will not state one point, as a fact, that I have not proven in dozens of instances. My wish is to so simplify this science that a child can understand it. My *demand* is, that this science be publicly recognized and adopted in our public schools, and that every child shall be given an opportunity to learn it. The great lack of the age is character reading. No one can understand or read another. We are constantly misunderstanding, and, consequently, drawing the wrong conclusion. Is it any wonder we have Bedlam where we ought to have Harmony?

CHAPTER XXI.

The Structure of the Hand.

In taking up Palmistry proper, as this system is based on the scientific principles of Physiology, therefore it is necessary for us to first note carefully the bone, muscle, nerve and blood development of the hand, and, as the hand, in turn, is a facsimile of the whole human body, and on its development depends our success in life, let us observe carefully for a moment the Structure, in the engraving No. 4.

In reading your hand, the palmist tells you the broad finger joints indicate a tendency to logic, system and order in work, a capacity for details and finish in what you do. The physiologist explains this by assuring you these large finger joints are needed for the attachment of well developed muscles, and that these latter give the steadiness required in exact and delicate movements. Thus, for

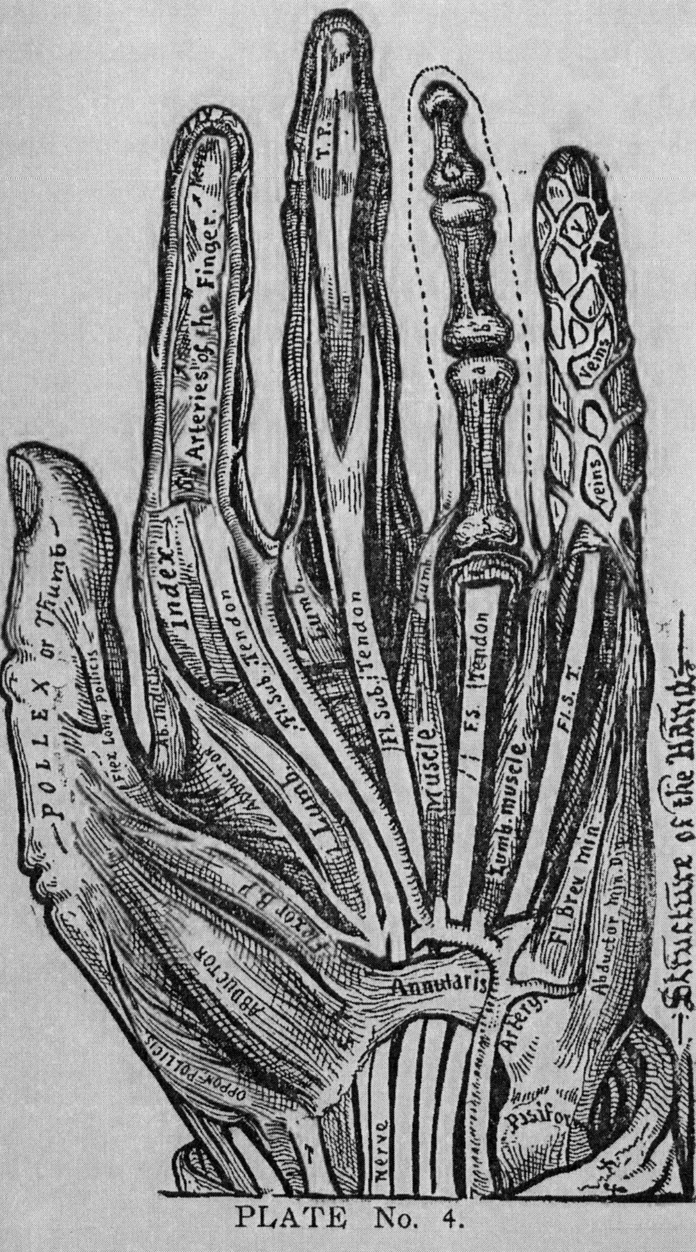
Arteries of the Finger.
T.P.
Veins
Veins
Index
Pollex or Thumb
Flex Long. Pollicis
Ab. Indicis
Abductor
Fl. Sub. Tendon
Lumb.
Fl. Sub. Tendon
Lumb.
Muscle
F.S. Tendon
Lumb. muscle
Fl. S. T.
Fl. Brev. min.
Abductor min. D.
Flexor B. P.
Abductor
Oppon. Pollicis
Annularis
Artery
Pisifor
Nerve
Structure of the Hand

PLATE No. 4.

every sign there is a scientific meaning. If your line of life is strong and well set in the palm of the hand, the physiologist will say, this indicates that you have a good bony and muscular system, and, therefore, strong powers of resistance against disease and death. The life line is formed by the muscles of the thnmb fastening on to the bone of the hand.

At the center of the wrist, we see the long tendons from the flexor muscles of the arm; these branch out to the fingers. The fourth finger, in the chart is dissected only deep enough to show the network of veins just below the skin; the middle finger shows only the tendons, as they fasten onto the joints; the arteries have been cut away, except a single branch, going to the first finger. Notice, the main arteries and nerves run around the side of the fingers. You will notice in engraving No. 5, the Chart of the Hand, the signs are printed on the sides of the fingers. Now, the nerves, as they polarize along the side of the fingers, deposit their energy. So, according to the fulness of the sides of the fingers would you read the faculty marked on each phalange. We say the wide, flat fingers will

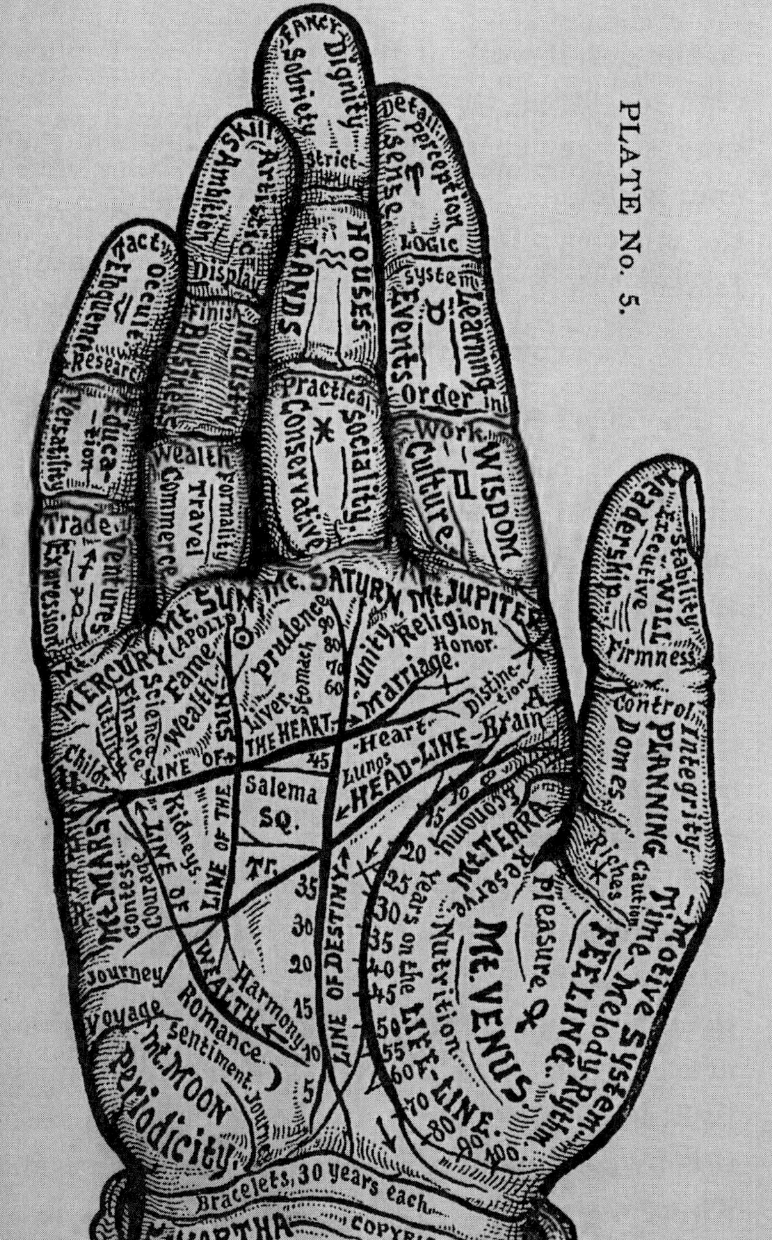
Fancy
Dignity
Sobriety
Strict
Detail
perception
sense
LOGIC
system
Learning
Events
Order
Skill
Ambition
Artistic
Display
Finish
Industry
Business
HOUSES
LANDS
Practical
Sociality
Conservative
Work
Culture
WISDOM
Tact
Eloquence
Occult
Research
Versatility
Educa-tion
Wealth
Commerce
Formality
Travel
Trade
Ventures
Expression
Stability
Leadership
Executive
WILL
Firmness
Mt. SUN (APOLLO)
Mt. SATURN
Mt. JUPITER
Mt. MERCURY
Fame
Wealth
Prudence
Religion
Honor
Unity
Marriage
Liver
Stomach
Science
Finance
Child
LINE OF SUN
THE HEART
Heart
Distinction
Brain
Lungs
HEAD-LINE
Control
Integrity
Domes
PLANNING
Salema SQ.
Kidneys
LINE OF THE
Tr.
Mt. MARS
Contest
Courage
LINE OF
Mt. TERRA
Economy
Reserve
Riches
Caution
Time
Motive
Years on the
Nutrition
Pleasure
Mt. VENUS
FEELING
Melody
Rythm
System
LINE OF DESTINY
LIFE-LINE
Journey
Voyage
WEALTH
Harmony
Romance
Sentiment
Mt. MOON
Periodicity
Bracelets, 30 years each
SIVARTHA COPYRIGHT
CHART OF THE HAND

PLATE No. 5.

do the detail work of the world. Detail work requires strength in the end of the fingers, so, we see, if the bone is large on the end, which is the case in broad finger tips, the muscles will be larger and more securely fastened than where the tips are pointed.

BREADTH AND CONCENTRATION.

The currents of nerve force accumulate intensity with the length of the tubules which they traverse; therefore, the longer the mental organs, the more intense, concentrated and brilliant are their functions. Wherever the organs are wide, and cover a greater lateral surface, there is greater diffusion of currents through the adjacent nerve cells. Therefore, breadth of the organs gives stability, permanence and diffusiveness in their functions. This vital law, of course, applies to the face and hands, as well as the brain. Even in the mineral world, the breadth of objects gives them the appearance of stability and permanence, while height gives the impression of lightness, elegance and mobility. We see this by comparing the pyramid and the palm. Thus, we see that long hands would possess

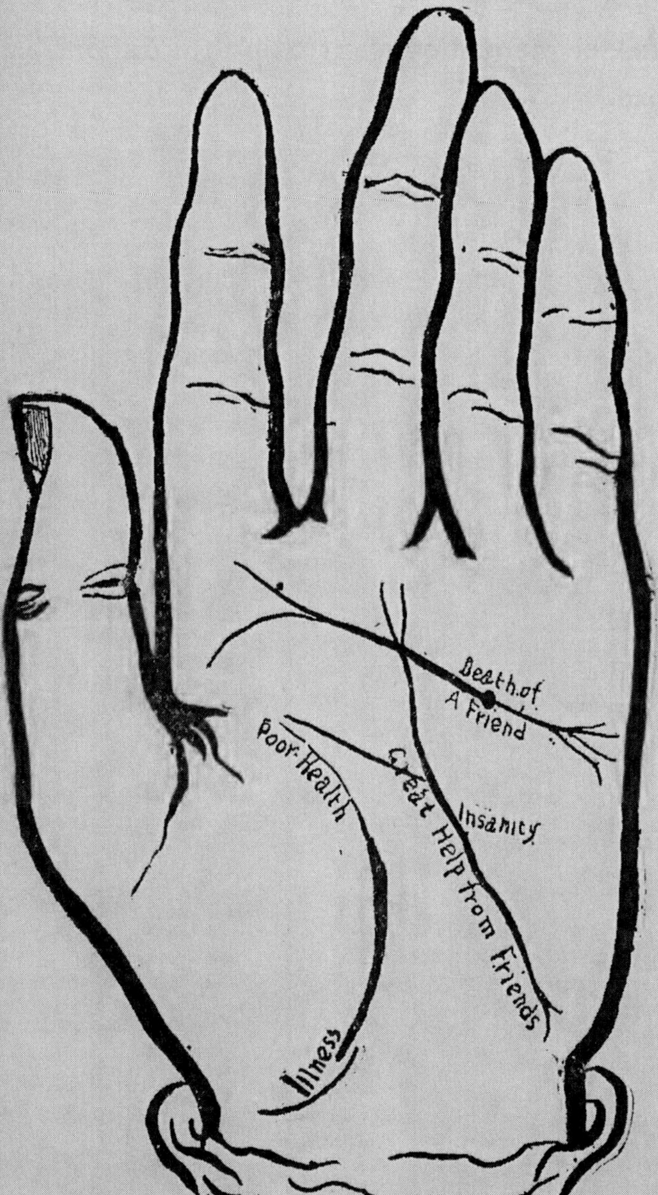

PHILOSOPHIC-HAND

PLATE No. 6.

greater mental concentration than short, broad ones.

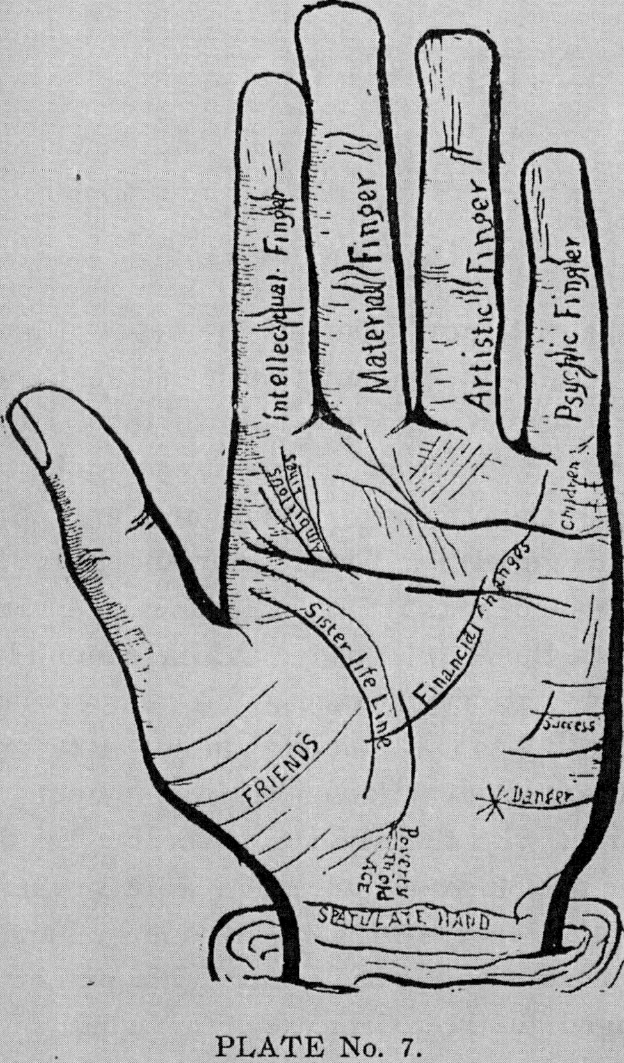
Intellectual Finger
Material Finger
Artistic Finger
Psychic Finger
Children
Sister Life Line
Financial Changes
Success
Danger
FRIENDS
SPATULATE HAND

PLATE No. 7.

CHAPTER XXII.

The Types of Hands.

We will now take up the types of hands. As a rule, the general form of the hand in each person corresponds with the head. A beautiful and well formed hand indicates a well balanced head and character. Broad hands go with a broad head and body. My experience is that the hand does not always follow the form of body; as I have found large people with small hands. The hand enlarges according to use, and one can tell, in this way, if the individual descended from parents who worked with their hands, or brains, or both. The person whose ancestors were workers in physical occupations will have large hands in proportion to his body, but if his parents belonged to the aristocracy, the hand will be small in proportion to the body and head.

Large hands are quite capable and inclined to do the skilled work of the world; they do not

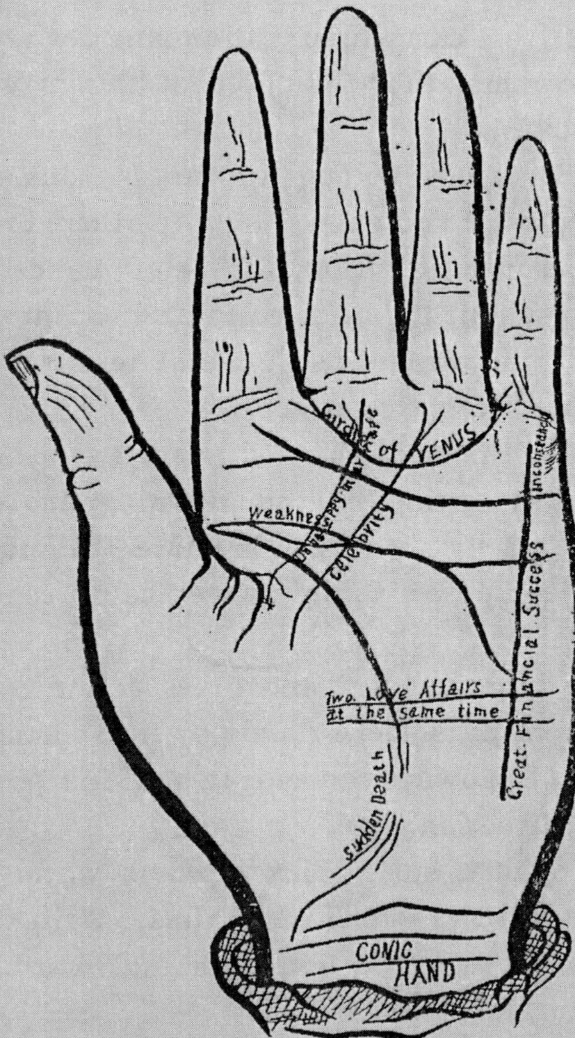
Girdle of VENUS
Inconstancy
Weakness
Celebrity
Great Financial Success
Two Love Affairs
at the same time
Sudden Death
CONIC
HAND

PLATE No. 8.

shrink from carrying out the plans devised by their owners; they take hold of things without gloves.

Small hands belong to the persons who plan colossal things and employ others to carry them into execution; the small hands dislike to submit to exact rules and minute details; their owners use general terms rather than precise statements.

It is to the medium sized hand that we must look for a display of both planning and executing; their owners appreciate the masses which compose a thing, as well as its constituent details.

The long, slender hand gives action, energy, strength, sincerity and power to command others; the owner concentrates all his powers in one direction.

The short, soft, thick hand is warm and hearty, always selfish in its aims. With thick skin, the owner is fitted for dull, hard, unthinking labor.

Hard hands have active power.

Soft hands have passive endurance.

The small, slender hand is the hand of literature, art and poetry; it shows, at least, a

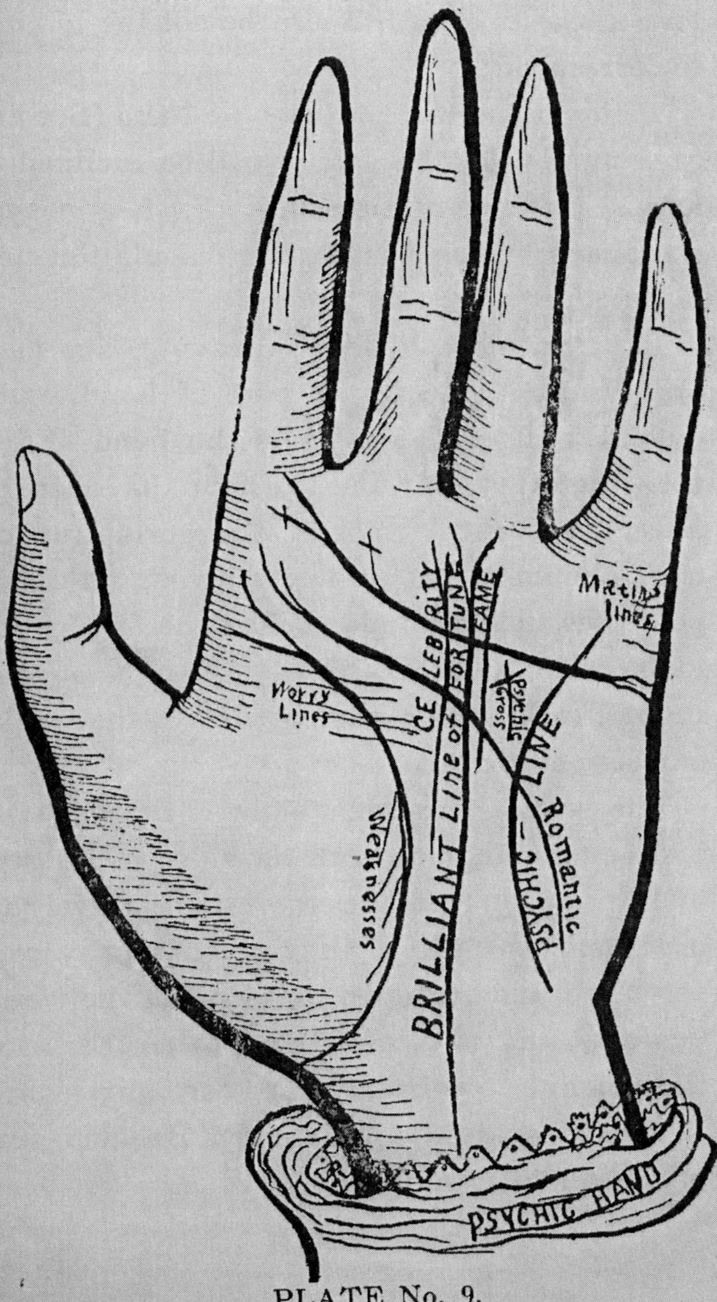
CELEBRITY
FORTUNE
FAME
Mating lines
Worry Lines
Psychic Cross
PSYCHIC LINE
BRILLIANT LINE of FORTUNE
Weaknesses
PSYCHIC – Romantic LINE
PSYCHIC HAND

PLATE No. 9.

love of these, even if there be not the talents to correspond.

With the knotty, philosophic hand (See engraving No. 6), the person will be inclined to logical methods of thinking. Such a person wants everything based upon calculation and knowledge.

The spatulate hand (Engraving No. 7) is broad across the upper part of hand, with wide flat finger tips; this is the hand of the active detail worker, also the hand that does the finest mechanical work of the world, and no child should be put into detail work unless it possesses such a hand. When the fingers are long, with a large third phalange of the thumb, called the Mount of Venus, they make our best musicians.

The square hand will show a square palm and square fingers, both on sides of fingers and tips; they possess perseverance, foresight, order and regularity; they are naturally conservative, and are noted for minding their own business, and wishing others to do the same; they incline to politeness and formality, while those with spatulate fingers seek freedom, simplicity and originality.

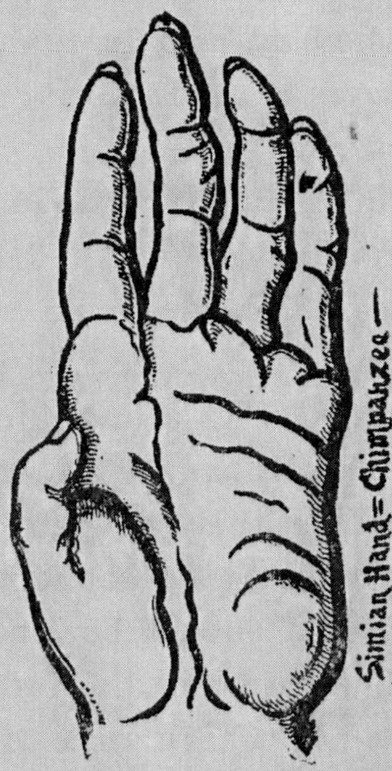

PLATE No. 10.

The artistic, or conical hand (Engraving No. 8) has the tips of the fingers rounded over the top like a thimble; the hand will be long and sometimes quite slender, more fully developed at the base of palm than the tip; they are great lovers of art in all its branches, fond of travel and change.

The psychic hand (Engraving No. 9) has delicate, tapering fingers and long, slender hands; the owner is ideal and mystic, dwelling in dreamland, inclined to prophecy and spiritual things; with a fine skin covering the inside of the hand, they will become poets and mediums. When this type shows large finger joints, they become philosophers.

A perfect hand should be elastic, firm and delicate. The thin, dry hand does not indicate or belong to a high state of health.

A soft, "mushy" hand that will seem like a lump of fat when you take it in your hand, is the indication of a character that will shirk responsibility; they are fond of dress and high living, but it will always be at the expense of others; they like to make a display of jewelry and fine clothes, also their feelings; they will weep with you and laugh with you, but do

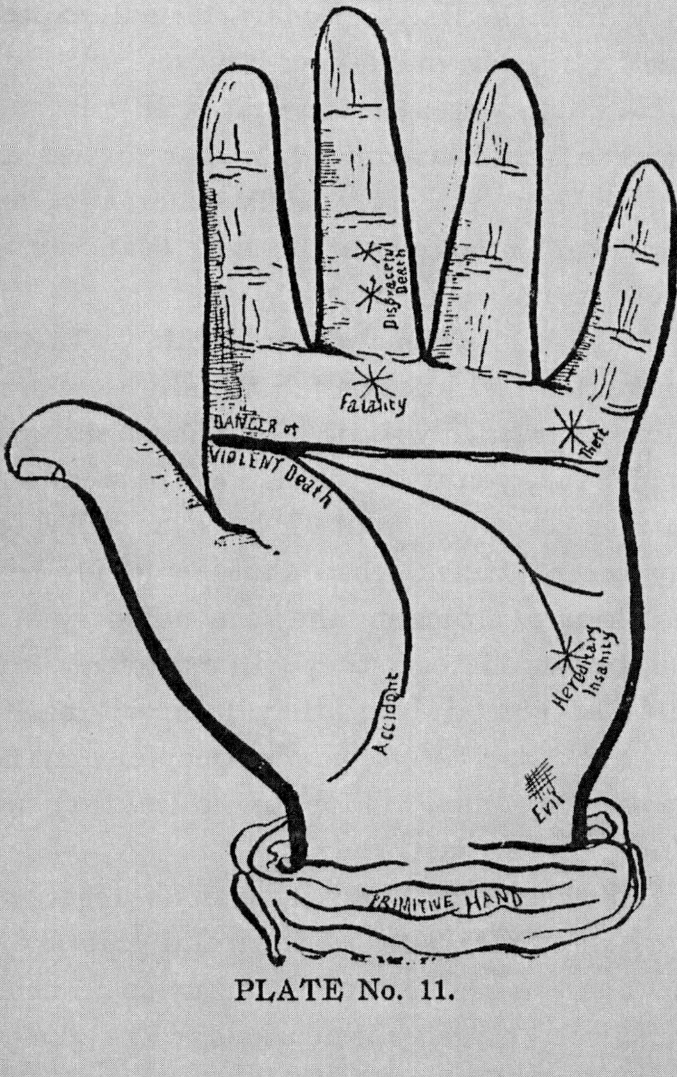
Disgraceful Death
Fatality
DANGER of
VIOLENT Death
Theft
Accident
Hereditary Insanity
Evil
PRIMITIVE HAND

PLATE No. 11.

not ask them for any cash, for on that mark they draw the line. A character will express itself very well in shaking hands.

Now take note: A man that will grip your hand so hard that you think your fingers are broken, is an intensely selfish character, and you want to look out or he will beat you on every turn.

The other extreme is very similar. In this shake there will not be felt the slightest pressure, their hand will lie like a dead thing in your hand, you will feel all sorts of weak sensations pass over you. I have actually felt my knees weaken when shaking hands with this kind of a person; they are not only selfish, but indifferent; they will expect you to do all the entertaining; they lack originality, and are conservative, narrow people; and, not having any thoughts for the future, they live chiefly in the past.

But the hand that will frankly meet you half way, with a firm but careful embrace is the one you can depend on in any or all emergencies; the are unpretentious, will make but little show of their feelings, but what they say will mean something.

Also take note of the way one carries his hands, when walking. A man whose hands ar tightly closed, will walk fast and his heels will come down hard, making a clicking sound, he will have an anxious, suspicious look. This man is close and stingy, and always on the lookout for someone to beat him.

But the man whose hands are flung carelessly open will have a springy, careless walk, a frank, open face. You would not hesitate to speak to him on the street nor to ask him for assistance, if you required it. Ladies, never address a strange man on the street without first noticing how he carries his hands, and, under no circumstances ask a favor of the man who carries his hands tightly closed.

The texture of the hand should be carefully noted. A delicate, elastic and well colored skin, a sensitive, refined nature; while a coarse, rough skin, a coarse, low nature.

The inside of a hand, as a whole, exerts attractive force; it is receptive, feminine; The back of the hand, on the contrary, radiates repulsive, or positive force; it is masculine. We use the inside of the hand in caressing, the back is used in striking. The sense of touch, the primary basis of all our feelings and senses, is far more developed on the inside; the back is less specialized, has far less detail in its signs.

CHAPTER XXIII.

Types and Expression of Thumbs.

Let us take up separately each finger and thumb. First, we will examine the thumb. It is the thumb of man which makes his hand so far superior to that of any lower animal. In the hand of the chimpanzee (Engraving No. 10), or any of the monkeys the great deficiency is in the thumb. It is small, weak, and quite incapable of acting with the fingers in any skilled work. The thumb, representing the faculties of will in the brain, gives originality and executive ability, according to its size and general development. Animals have but little originality. You know the old saying, "Monkey see, monkey do." A person with a small thumb will, therefore, lack in originality, and will be but an echo of others, as in the primitive thumb (Engraving No. 11).

So you see the importance of well developed thumbs, for you may have ever so well developed an intellect, if your will is deficient, you will lack the power to demonstrate or execute your knowledge. I believe anyone can strengthen, or call into greater activity, any or all of the faculties, by constantly appealing to any one or all for greater expression; for as the muscles are developed by constant exercise of them, so are the faculties by like process. If we do not use a muscle, it soon becomes dormant and useless, and so with our faculties. Use will power, and we will develop thumbs, and become better men and women.

The root of the thumb forms the Mount of Venus. It is the seat of feeling, as we shall see later. The middle phalange indicates the practical ability to reason, plan and scheme, and, on the back, the integrity needed to carry out the plans. The breadth of the first joint gives the sustaining power of self control; the first phalange gives stability, executive talent and the qualities of leadership. If this phalange is short and weak, the person will be ruled by others, and will lack in firmness, when an appeal is made to the heart, easily led through their affections, even against their better judgment. As a whole, the thumb indicates the power of the individual life to express itself in outward conduct. Hence, at its base, we find the line of life. When the first phalange is short, and the middle one is long, they will have energy without order, impulse without judgment, and are apt to be rash and arbitrary.

Now, observe the many peculiar shapes and kinds of thumbs we meet. A thumb short in the first phalange, and bending far back (Engraving No. 11), is a great spendthrift; will have but little, if any, idea of economy, as a rule; light hearted and easily led. A large thumb, well developed in both phalanges, with a tendency to bend toward the hand, will be domineering, tyrannical, a cruel master, and an exacting husband and father. But a large thumb, well balanced, standing straight, or slightly bending back, will be self reliant, and if the finger tips are square or spatulate, and the joints knotty, he will be fond of the exact sciences, and the occupations derived from them, as engineering, architecture, and the teaching of the higher mathematics.

Notice the difference between the right and left thumb. You will many times find a small thumb on the left hand, and a large thumb on the right. This will show the person has developed his or her Will since a child, as the left hand shows the character of the child, as it never changes its proportions. You will many times find an entirely different hand in the right—sometimes better and sometimes worse. When better, you know they have had good environments, and have taken advantage of them; when worse, the opposite would be true. A fine skin will always redeem, to a certain extent, bad qualities in the thumb, or in any other part of the hand.

THE STANDARD MEASURE OF THE THUMB.

The thumb of the right hand should measure close, if not quite, to the second joint of the first finger. A thumb measuring beyond this joint would indicate ungovernable temper, furious impulses; one of the characteristics of murderers, highwaymen, wife beaters, and brutal parents. Sometimes its shape is almost clubbed; this increases all the detestable signs above enumerated. The thumb with the middle phalange slightly concave indicates a brilliant intellect, quick, sharp and deep.

It might be interesting to state, dear reader, that I have found the above statements to be absolutely true. In the three prisons which I visited in California where I read over three hundred criminals, from the common petty thief to the murderer, in every instance I found something wrong in the thumb. In every case, the petty thief will show a small thumb, a long, slender palm and short, stubby fingers. The murderer will show an extremely large thumb, with a great length in the first phalange; in a few cases, these thumbs measured almost to the first joint of the forefinger; they will have a thick, heavy palm, with a heavy development on the side of the hand, which would indicate courage, as we shall see when we study the palm. Now, by an intellectual observation on the part of parents and teachers, this condition could be changed in the child. I claim, by all the rights of common sen se, society is to blame for its criminals, for they are no phenomena, but are the result of causes, which society recognizes but refuses to remove. In the first place it takes generations to build a criminal. He must have his environments, for, like the rose, without his especial conditions, he could not develop. Continue the system of competition that develops all the low, ferocious, animal faculties in the brain of man, and society will continue to bring forth its crop of criminals. Every year the crop increases, and we build larger prisons and erect more scaffolds. Ye gods! where is the end?

We will close this review of the thumb with an extract from Saint Germaine.

"Gallileo, Descartes and Newton had very large thumbs; Voltaire also had an enormous one. The first phalange of the French martyr King, the weak, vacillating Louis XVI, was very small; on the other hand, Cretins, and other idiots, have but slightly developed thumbs. It has been noticed in idiots, that, until by suitable treatment, rays of intelligence are drawn from them, they constantly keep their hands shut, with the fingers above the thumb; in proportion as their minds expand, the thumb comes out of its hiding place, until, when the hand is closed, the thumb is outside."

I have also heard it remarked, that when a person is about to die, the hand will close over the thumb, and it is looked upon as a sure sign of death, and when this occurs, unless their will can be aroused, the soul soon departs.

This is also observed in infants. The thumb is weak, and is usually held covered by fingers in the center of palm. As the will develops, the thumb will grow stronger, until when the hands close the thumb will be outside. The general character can be read in the formation of the infant's hand, and that is the time to read it, and then train it accordingly.

CHAPTER XXIV.

Types and Expression of Fingers.

In taking up the study of the fingers, the student will do well to note this lesson carefully. The fingers represent the faculties of the intellect, and again, so much depends on having a well developed intellect, not in a few of the faculties, but in all. The faculty of dignity, which is shown in the first phalange of the second finger, is one that should receive especial attention, for if the child or person lack in this faculty, they will continually underestimate themselves. Remember, society will estimate the individual at the price he sets on himself.

I should also mention the faculty of *venture* and *hope* and *caution*, also *sense*, which indicates the power to analyze what you have perceived. You will find, many times, perception large, while sense to analyze what they have perceived will be small. In such a case, the the child should be taught to use its analyzing powers. Teachers and parents usually class the children all together, not knowing how to differentiate. The result is, nine times out of ten, the child gets the wrong training. Now, a little light, such as palmistry could throw on the subject, would change this haphazard condition to the great benefit of all concerned.

The first, or index, finger is used to direct the tool or instrument in many kinds of skilled work, hence its nerve force comes chiefly from the intellect in the brain; this determines its meaning. The sense of touch and general perception is connected with the first phalange. This sense is the basis of all our physical knowledge. The middle phalange gives the capacity for general learning; and the third gives us practical wisdom in its application. On each finger, we have marked its general qualities. Where those give breadth to the joint, the word is printed across the finger, as the words "logic, strictness and display," etc.; this breadth at the first joint of the forefinger indicates mental order and logical power. The length of the first phalange shows power of perception;

with a pointed tip, keenness of perception. Breadth at the second joint shows order in work. The word is placed lengthwise whenever the quality gives length to phalange between the joints. These finger signs can all be learned from the chart.

We see that the length of each phalange indicates different qualities from its breadth, yet the two are closely related in each case; logic and system, which are indicated by the breadth, must be based on learning and events, which are indicated in the length, and this is shown by their relative places on the fingers.

Looking at the chart of the hand (Engraving No. 5), the breadth of the first joint of the first finger indicates logic. This is an intellectual phase in the corresponding place of the middle finger. This breadth means strictness and propriety in our social behavior; its meaning is now social instead of intellectual. On the third finger, this breadth indicates the love of display, the power to finish and beautify the work we are doing. It has now become a faculty of the will in the finger. The breadth in the fourth finger gives us the power of thought, and a tendency to look deep into things. Below this, at the next joint, what is order in work in the first finger, becomes the tendency to be practical in the second; in the third, it gives the instincts for accumulating wealth, and, in the fourth; a talent for financial transactions.

Three mental phases are shown by the first, second and third phalanges of the fingers: the first indicates the intuitive perceptions, or spiritual phase; the second phalanges express the phase of learning, truth and reason, and the third gives the material, practical and lower instincts. Thus, as we go from the palm to the tips of the fingers, we are passing to qualities of higher, and higher order.

Again, the first finger is called the intellectual; the second, the physical; the third, the artistic; the fourth, the psychic. Note the length of the first phalange of the third finger, as this gives the skill required in art. Notice the way you hold a brush or pen; you will find this phalange gives the steadying power to the instrument used. Language is shown in the first phalange of the fourth finger. Medium language brings the tip of the little finger to the first joint of the third finger; above or below would indicate small or large language.

Now, let us note, for a few moments, the finger tips. According to the teachers and old masters in palmistry, we may look for but four kinds of finger tips (I have found no more in my practice). These are as follows: pointed, conical, square and spatulate. Sometimes we find two or more of these types on one hand. A mixed type of finger tips is always best, as it would indicate that the person could master more than one kind of work. The best mixed type of finger tips is a pointed forefinger, a spatulate second, a conical third and a square fourth. I am referring to the tips only in this reference, as the pointed forefinger gives us keen perception; the spatulate second, adaptability for detail work, with great activity; a conical third finger, artistic skill and a strong sense of the beautiful, and a square fourth, for common sense, close reasoning, and speech, ready and to the point. The rarest type found to prevail in the whole hand is the pointed tips; thus, when it does occur, it makes the person a dreamer, a poet, an idealist, an artist, a composer, a philosopher. With these, the soul rules over matter and has only contempt for the wretched necessities and meannesses of an earthly existence; he is in the world, but not of the world. They are the fingers of the early Christian martyrs; they are found in the mysterious convents, where breathes yet the intense religious idealism of the middle ages.

The owner of conical fingers is attracted by beautiful ideas, beautiful things, lovely landscapes, great books or works of art. They are charitable and unselfish. The owners of these fingers are not made for an ordinary life, and in married life are often a failure. They are warm, generous and sometimes inconstant.

The square type of fingers indicates perseverance, foresight, order and regularity. It is the hand of a thorough business man, the hand of the law-abiding citizen, of the steady plodder and the speculator. He is a model bookkeeper, a cashier of integrity, and as good pay as he expects to be paid. He will mind his own business, and will expect others to do the same.

THE SPATULATE FINGERS.

The spatula is a little instrument used by druggists, in some of their operations, having the tip slightly wider than the body; and in this shape does the nailed phalange end in this type. (See Engraving No. 7.) It is invariably the characteristic of action, energy and quick and constant movement. A hard palm will be the complement of this type of fingers; the thumb will be large. If well shaped, a hand may be read as follows: self-confidence, a desire for abundant means, very enthusiastic, fondness for outdoor sports, for agricultural occupations, for mathematics, and the theory of war. They are conquerors and fighters, and fond of authority; they are very liberal in religion, and they are undoubtedly the makers of our present civilization.

Now, a word as to the nails. The finger nails indicate both health and character, Long nails show less physical strength than short and broad ones. If long, and also fluted and ribbed, they show a tendency to lung troubles. Persons with long nails have more calmness, gentleness, self-control than those with short nails. Filbert shaped nails go with the conical, artistic hand. Thin, small nails indicate delicate, or feeble health. Round nails go with a hand fond of luxury and pleasure. At the base of the nails, large moons indicate a good circulation. Short nailed persons are critical and fault finding. Spots on the nails indicate nervous excitability. Short nails, pointed at the base, warn us of heart trouble. In perfect mental and physical health, the color of the nails should be a delicate pink, without spots, and the moon well developed at the root.

CHAPTER XXV.

The Mounts of the Hand.

This lesson takes up the palm of the hand. Now, the palm represents the emotional faculties in the brain. The palm is said to be the battle ground of life. Of a truth, the lines that cross its surface do give us a very clear outline of the changes and events of life. As we will see, under its proper head, the palm is divided into nine different parts, and each part is named after its ruling planet. How do the planets have anything to do with our hands? In this way: the hand, as well as all other parts of the body, is builded by the brain. The magnetic currents from Solar Systems, or Signs, and all the planets in our own Solar System play upon the brain, and, according to their force, develop, or change, the faculties in the brain. The part of the hand which polarizes the nerves descending from the faculties Jupiter rules will naturally show the strength of Jupiter, and so of the others. Even the signs have their especial polarity in the hand, as we shall see in its place.

The Mounts of the Hand are the fleshy pads at the the base of the thumb and of each finger, and in the palm. They are named as follows: Venus, Jupiter, Saturn, the Sun, Mercury, Mars, the Moon, and Terra, or Earth.

Mount Venus, at the base of the thumb, gives warmth of affection, gentleness, kindness, admiration for beauty and grace, melody and music, sense of rythm and time, and a desire for pleasure and society. Persons with this mount large are interested in poetry, painting and music, but the special talents for these are indicated in the fingers. We may love art, yet not be able to execute. The absence of this mount indicates coldness and dullness in matters of art, with all the passions selfish and dry. Many lines on this mount denote great warmth of temperament.

Mount Terra, or the Earth, is marked at the upper part of the thumb's base. It gives a love and capacity for acquiring and using wealth, with physical enjoyment of the earth and its beauties, as well as its utilities. It is the complement of both Venus and Mount Jupiter.

Mount Jupiter is at the base of the forefinger. It gives reason in religion, a high sense of honor and social unity, a feeling that the mind and brain should rule the body of the animal man. With this mount large, the person is inclined to display and ceremony, and delights in entertaining others. The person is usually well built. and generally handsome. With square fingers, the person has a great love of regularity and established authority; with a well developed second finger and a good Mount of Saturn, the success in life and the good fortune of the subject is assured. Large mounts of Jupiter and the Moon make the person honorable, placid and just; with a large Mount of Mercury, the person would make a good physician.

Mount Saturn gives a character marked by prudence and natural caution, with a tendency toward such pursuits as agriculture, horticulture or mineralogy. The person with this mount large has a natural attraction to the earth. He is self centered and self confident, and can enjoy his own company.

Mount Apollo, or the Sun, endows a person with instincts of art; it tends to success, glory, fame and brilliancy of fortune. This mount large denotes genius, intelligence, tolerance and wealth; the love is more affectionate than sensual; the person is imitative and inventive, with a talent for discovery; the temper is quick, though not lasting or spiteful.

Mount Mercury gives a tendency to science, spirit, eloquence and expression; it shows a capacity for commerce, speculation, adventure and industry, with agility and promptitude in thought and action combined. With Mount Saturn, it imparts a sobriety, a certain practical, intuitive sense, which foretells success.

Mount Mars is at the side of the hand, between Mercury and the Moon. It gives courage, resolution, contest and a strong capacity for command; combined with Mount Apollo, it gives order and energy in art, great perseverance and truth in action. Men with this mount large are apt to marry women of the Venus type.

The Mount of the Moon gives periodicity of thought, feeling and action. The moon is the clock of our Solar System; its exactly measured phases have made it the standard of time amongst all nations; it cannot, therefore, denote inconstancy and capricious changes, as the palmists wrongly imagined. This mount does give love of changes, but of methodical and definite ones. This is widely different from inconstancy. This mount gives large imagination, sentiment, romance, love of mystery, poetry of soul and charity of thought. In music, it tends to harmony, rather than melody. The person with it large will be fond of voyages and travel. With a well marked mystic cross in the quadrangle, the person will have the faculty of spiritual vision.

It will be noticed that in general a mount expresses similar qualities to those of the finger of which it is the base. The fingers give detail to the expression in each quality. The quadrangle is the space in the palm between the head and heart line. The triangle is the space between head line and line of life.

In the center of the palm, the quadrangle, the triangle, and the palm, by their fulness, give support to qualities which belong to the lines which cross them. A full palm is, therefore, an indication of good vitality of action and nutrition. They keep what they get. The hollow palm will not hold its substance well; they will part with their money and vitality easily. They are not so fortunate in life as the one with a full palm.

Our physical attractions to the earth are marked on the upper part of Mount Venus, as Mount Terra. This is shown on the general chart.

On each phalange of the finger, the fleshy part, by its fulness and prominence, indicates the abundance of vital force, and the activity which belongs to that particular part of the finger.

If a mount is much covered with lines, this is thought to indicate an excessive, or over abundant development of its qualities. A single line upon a mount gives emphasis to its qualities, and is thus a fortunate sign. A line which gives out three branches is regarded as the best indication. Lines which cut across a mount warn us of obstacles, and what the obstacles may be, we can judge from the character of the mount; thus, on the Mount of Mercury, they would indicate obstacles in commercial business; on Mount Jupiter, the cross line would mean hinderances to our ambition and elevation, but if the ascending line is deeper than the cross line, then the evil omens of the cross lines are neutralized and destroyed. It is very necessary that each mount should be located under each finger. The apex of the mount can be located, if not by the naked eye, with the aid of a magnifying glass. When the mount is doing its best work, it will be mediumly well developed, and firm under the pressure of the finger; when too large, and of a soft quality, the individual has not made use of his natural ability. The apex of the mount, wherever located, will present an appearance like this:

If you find the apex of Jupiter square under the finger, Jupiter would be a ruling planet at birth; but if this apex is between the fingers, it would indicate you would be fifty years of age before Jupiter would be ruling. Divide up the space, and you can get at the exact date when a planet will be giving its strongest influence. This reasoning will hold good for Jupiter, Saturn, Sun and Mercury, but the other mounts or planets you must judge by their fulness—the fuller a mount, the stronger its power.

CHAPTER XXVI.

The Major Lines of the Hand.

The major lines of the hand are three in number: the line of life, the line of the heart, and the line of the head. These all begin on the upper side of the hand.

In the chart, the scale of years is marked on the line of life, showing how long each person's life will extend. If the line commences under the Mount of Jupiter, great ambition, often great honors and success. (Very sure.) Chained under the Mount of Jupiter, bad health in early life. Chained or linked, delicacy of constitution; of various thicknesses throughout its course, capricious and fickle temper; thin or laddered in the center,ill health during that portion of life. A spot terminating this thinness, sudden death. The line of life should be long, so as to encircle the Mount of Venus; it should be strong and clear, without breaks or cross lines. Then it denotes a long life and good health, with a good character and disposition. If pale and broad, it indicates ill health, with a feeble and envious character. A break in the line always denotes an illness, when the line is broken in both hands, there is great danger of death. The shorter the line, the shorter the life. At the point at which the line terminates in both hands may be foretold the time at which death will supervene; if the break is only in one hand, then the person will recover; if the line ceases abruptly, with a few little parallel lines, it foretells a sudden death. All these signs are illustrated in the charts. The line of life may be strengthened and enforced by a sister line, that is, another line lying close along, and parallel with, the principal line. The sister lines may be found with any of the lines, always giving increased power of the same kind. Rays across the line of life to the palm denote worries and troubles. If the line be tasselled at the extremity, it means poverty and loss of money late in life. A fork in the very center of the line is a warning of diminished vital force.

The line of the heart was called the mensal, or mental, line by the ancients. It belongs to those aspects of affection which are more intellectual in their character, more connected with our mental life and knowledge, than are the feelings indicated by Mount Venus. When the line of the heart is of a good color, and clearly traced, the person has an affectionate disposition, a good and upright heart, an equable temper and good health. This line is best when it rises in three branches on the Mount of Jupiter. If it arises under Saturn, the love will be of a more physical type. When this line turns up to Mercury, the love will be inclined to instability; if it turns down to Mars, that means jealousy and quarrels. The absence of the heart line means bad faith, wickedness and liability to an early death. A break in the heart line may mean weakness, and, consequently, a broken engagement or a rupture with one we love. The cause may be found by the place of the break. If under Saturn, the cause of the break is fate; nearer the Sun, the cause is folly; under Mercury, it is avarice or ignorance. A secondary heart line is sometimes found, and is called the "Girdle of Venus." It simply intensifies the qualities and tendencies shown in the heart line.

The line of the head is normally joined to the line of life at the commencement. When well formed, clear and strong, it denotes good sense, clear judgment and self mastery. This is the line which acts as a clear and accurate gauge to the intellectual worth of the subject, and to the healthy condition of his or her brain and blood circulation. It is often called, on that account, "the Cerebral." The line is found under the line of the heart, more or less parallel to it, separated from it by what is called "the Quadrangle," and generally, when normal, connected, at its starting point, with the line of life. If the head line only commences under the Mount of Saturn, then it indicates a late development of the intellectual faculties; if long, straight and clear, common sense; if the line is chained and uneven, it betrays unsettled convictions; chained or linked, headaches. Spots on the head line also indicate headaches, and if the stomach is weak, sick headaches. A head line that turns down to the Mount of the Moon, running well onto the mount, is an indication of insanity; if a star is on the end of the line, hereditary insanity. This is especially true when the individual has pointed fingers and a fine skin. Out of sixty insane people I examined in one day, only four had other than pointed finger tips. Society should pay great attention to this point. Parents, if you have a child with long, pointed fingers, a fine skin, and a large Mount of the Moon and Venus, you have been intrusted with the finest of organizations, and you should take great care to protect it against the inharmonies of life. There is a terrible strain on the brain of such sensitive children or people, when not understood and forced to do the detail work that belongs to the spatulate or square handed. It is not surprising to me that such men and women, under trying conditions, lose their mental balance. Imagine a woman of this fine psychic, poetic nature, surrounded with four or five children, for whom she must sew, wash, cook and mend,—all detail occupations which she cannot do well. The result will be, failure on her part to keep things going. Her spatulate fingered neighbor will laugh at her, and call her lazy; her husband will become tired of his untidy home and half cooked meals; the children, not being properly trained, will grow more and more unmanageable, and the poor mother, whose only fault is, not understanding herself, nor being understood by others, at last, breaks down under the strain, and is carted to the insane asylum.

Nature is a wise mother, so she carefully prepares each child for his special work in life. If we go to work, in our blind ignorance, and apply the wrong training, we must take the consequences in the form of misspent lives. No attention is paid to the child, as to whether it is adapted to its occupation by nature, or not. The mechanic is often pushed into the pulpit, and the natural born orator trained to do the mechanical work. Is it any wonder that the preacher makes a failure as a preacher, and the mechanic gets tired of his job?

If the head line sends branches up toward Jupiter, it shows that the person is easily wounded in his self love; if such branches turn toward Saturn, they mean legacies or future possessions; if toward Mercury, commercial success; toward Venus, it shows that the person's intellect will be easily warped by losses or friends. When the head line sends a decided branch down to the Mount of the Moon, it shows tendencies to romance, and, with a small Mount of Jupiter, it shows a deceitful character. If there be two head lines, it is a sure sign of good fortune and inheritance. If one goes to the Mount of the Moon, it indicates a kind of double life, spiritual and physical.

Some writers have held that these lines of life, head and heart could have no such meanings, because they are produced by the natural folding or closing of the hand. We may grant that this is the direct cause, but let us ask if this very folding and closing is not for the purpose of doing the varied work, and expressing the myriad thoughts which make up our lives? Truly, if the movements have significance, the lines must have it also.

CHAPTER XXVII.

The Minor Lines of the Hand.

The minor lines are also three in number, the line of destiny, the line of wealth,and the line of brilliancy or distinction. On the chart ot types are given many variations of the lines from their normal positions and forms, with what each of these variations would indicate. Of course, we would not find all these variations on any one hand; they are placed together for greater convenience of study.

The line of destiny, or of Saturn, may start from any one of three principle points, it should normally end on the Mount of Saturn, and begin near the first bracelet; thus its most natural course is along the most central line of vital force and action in the hand, and this is why it indicates the general destiny or fortune. Following this course, it indicates good success in life. If the line of destiny start from the line of life, it signifies that success in life is due to our own personal effort. If the line start from the Mount of the Moon, it indicates that, to a certain extent, the fortune is derived from the caprice of the opposite sex. A branch from the Mount of the Moon to the line of destiny, points to long journeys or the desire for them. If the destiny line commences faintly and then becomes more clear, it foretells a better ending than its beginning, and the reverse is also true. The line, if twisted at the base and straight at the top, indicates early misfortunes, with good luck later in life. A twisted condition of the line is said to denote quarrels. To count age on this line, study the chart. The age at which an event occurs, as shown by the breaks on the line, may be predicted with certainty. The absence of the fate line denotes a self made life.

The line of brilliancy, Sun, or Apollo, may commence at the line of life, the Plain of Mars, or the Mount of the Moon. Its presence points to glory, distinction, celebrity, art, wealth, merit or success in life. It is best when found neat and straight, ending upon the Mount of Apollo in a single line or three branches. With the Mounts of Mercury and Jupiter well developed, this line is regarded as a certain indication of wealth, and such a person will become celebrated by his fortune, dignity and merit, not less than by his talents or scientific capacities. Cross lines on the Mount of the Sun indicate obstacles which stand in the way of success. If the lines form stars on the mount, this shows good fortune from the favors of friends, or from the help of others.

The line of wealth may commence from the line of life, the line of destiny, or the Mount of the Moon. It should normally end on the Mount of Mercury. When this line begins at the line of life, it indicates the child would earn his own living. At the date at which this line crosses the destiny line will show when he started for himself; but if the line start from the Mount of the Moon, or the center of palm, he will be assisted financially by others. Wherever the line breaks will show a change in finance. If it should grow stronger, as it ascends from the break, the change would be counted a good one; if weaker, a poor one. Look opposite on the destiny line for the scale of dates, as this line governs dates on the sun and wealth lines.

MARRIAGE LINES.

In the olden days, wives were bought and sold like any other piece of merchandise; therefore, it became the custom among palmisters to foretell marriage from the Mount of Mercury; the horizontal lines meaning marriage—for instance, two lines, two marriages —the perpendicular lines indicating children. I have found these lines very satisfactory in my practice.

In studying these lines, always consult the right hand. To get the dates correct, first examine the life line, and, after determining the age the person will live to, apply in this manner: if the person will live to eighty, call the space from the heart line to the root of little finger eighty years, now divide up the space, and count the line nearest the root of the little finger the first date. In this manner, one can predict with almost certainty the date. These lines do not always indicate a marriage. Nature knows no man made ceremony, she simply chronicles the mating dates, when one is more inclined toward the marriage or mating state. Quite often these lines appear when one is already married. If there is harmony existing between them, this condition will only intensify the harmony, but if there be inharmony, then look out for a separation. This has been my experience. Right here comes in the value of the Signs of the Zodiac in advising people in selecting partners who will be suitable to their temperament, or in explaining how to get along better with the one they have. The children that will live will show strong, well developed perpendicular lines; the weak lines are not liable to live, except in cases where the Sun is a ruling planet. I have then found weak lines have developed into strong children. Crosses on branches of heart line show brilliant marriages.

CHAPTER XXVIII.

The Variant Lines.

The chance lines, or the variants, which are of the most importance are given in our charts. In judging of these lines, and of all the variations and changes in the principle lines, the student must exercise his own good sense, as the variations themselves all take place according to law. The lines are seldom found alike in any two persons. Because Apollo represents fortune, and Venus, love, therefore we infer that a chance line from Venus to Apollo indicates a fortunate marriage, as marked in the chart. We simply combine the influence of the two mounts, or the two parts which the line may connect, and draw our inference as to what the combination will produce. Thus, as Mount Mars is strength for contest, and Venus, for love, we infer that two parallel lines from Venus to Mars indicate a strife between two love affairs which are carried on at the same time.

On the Mount of Venus, we may find long, curved lines, which appear to run parallel to the line of life. These minor life lines are thought to indicate the number of friends, or intimate associates, who have more or less deeply influenced our course of life. If these parallel lines touch the line of life, they would indicate a true friendship, or one to be relied upon in an emergency. Lines which cut across these indicate disturbed relations.

A single line on Mount Mercury indicates modesty and moderation, and, in many instances, a strange and unexpected stroke of good fortune.

Horizontal lines cutting the Mount of Mars and the Moon, beginning under the heart line, indicate travels by land; perpendicular lines, travels by water. The shorter the line, the shorter the journey.

If, at the quadrangle, the lines of heart and head are widely separated, generosity of feelings and a liberal giver; but if the line of the heart descends to the head line, it denotes egotism and selfishness. If the head line and heart line unite under the first finger, it is the sign of great danger threatening life; if in both hands, it presages a sudden and violent death. This is not true unless the life line also breaks, and where it breaks will give you the date of death. Always be careful in predicting death, as some people receive suggestions of such a character in a detrimental manner. I have had to correct many mistakes made by amateur palmists, who had come to a conclusion at once on some such a point, without weighing the evidence against it. All palmists should understand the power of suggestion, as we can do a great deal of good by giving the right suggestion, and the opposite is also true.

In locating dates on heart or head line, proceed the same as with marriage line, taking length of life line as your gauge. If the life line measures seventy-five, then the head or heart line will be counted the same.

A straight line from the Moon to Mercury indicates good fortune; a curved line from the Moon to Mercury shows occult powers and capacity for visions and presentiments. The occult tendencies, in the line of research, are shown by parallel lines on the middle phalange of the fourth finger.

Lines which start from the line of life and run up toward Jupiter or Saturn indicate self help, or efforts put forward to better our condition mentally or physically.

The bracelets, or horizontal lines at the wrist, are each regarded as indicating thirty years of life. They are thus echoes of the life line.

CHAPTER XXIX.

Crosses, Stars and Triangles.

Each of these have meanings, according to their position. A star on Mount Jupiter means that we shall gain our love or our ambition. Two stars on Pisces (the third phalange of the second finger) means a shameful death. A star on the heart line means the death of some near relative; on middle of thumb, in a woman, foretells riches and fortune through marriage. On Mount Saturn a star generally indicates a bad fatality. We must take care, and not mistake a cross for a star.

A cross on Mount Jupiter points to a happy marriage; in the quadrangle, it is called the mystic cross, and shows that the person is inclined to mysticism and religion. If this cross is joined to the line of destiny, it foretells a good fortune arising from religion or from the use of occult powers.

In all true and natural symbolism, the cross

The Cross.—Polar forces united; a change; on branch of Heart line, Mairrage.

The Star.—On Jupiter or Apollo. Distinction; a certain or fatal event.

The Square.—A plan of action or of life: protection: strength.

The Triangle.—Aptitude for science: diplomacy: exactness.

The Circle.—On Apollo, glory: on a line, an injury.

The Island.—Weakness: disease: a turning aside: division.

The Grille.—Obstacles: faults: confusion: excesses.

The Spot.—Black or blue, a disease: red, a wound: white some good.

Chained Line.—Obstacles, irregularities.

Broken Line.—Interruptions: illness.

Tasseled Lines.—Feebleness: waste.

Sister Lines.—Increased power.

PLATE No. 12. CHART MARKS.

Samples of each hierograph, with their general meanings.

signifies construction, the sex forces and life principles. The ancient Romans did an infernal thing when they used the cross for punishment in crucifixion, but their evil perversion of this symbol did not change the law and truth of nature, and we must accept nature's meaning in the study of palmistry. The cross is not a sign of evil, but it does indicate the changes which come from the union of two forces. Of these changes, marriage is the greatest.

The grille consists of a number of lines crossing each other, like the utensil from which it is named. It is generally an indication of obstacles, or of faults which belong to the mount on which it is found.

The triangle always denotes an aptitude for science. It may be formed neatly by itself, or made by the chance coincidence of three lines. On Mount Jupiter, the triangle shows diplomatic ability; on Apollo, it indicates science applied to art; on Mercury, talent in politics; on Mars, it shows science in war; on Venus, calculation and interest in love matters, and on Saturn, science in agricultural and horticultural lines of work.

The square is an index of power and energy in those qualities which are proper to the mount or line on which they are found. The square represents good sense, organization, plans of action and means of protection. It may either be a neat figure by itself, or it may be formed by the crossing of principle or cross lines. If it encloses a bad sign, it protects the person from the evil effects which would otherwise be indicated. They are certainly a symbol of plans, though the palmists have not noted this fact, and we may judge what was the nature of the plan by the mount on which it is found. A square in the quadrangle indicates a reformer.

An island may mean one of three things: either it betrays some hereditary evil; or it means an interruption, an obstacle; or it is a sign of something disgraceful. For instance, an island on the head line shows a hereditary weakness of the head; if it is on the heart line, it reveals hereditary heart disease. In a bad hand, this might signify an illicit love. On the upper part of the line of life, an island indicates some mystery connected with the person's birth, or poor health in early life.

From a star on Mount Venus, a line which crosses over to the head line shows a deep disappointment in love. A line from Venus across to Mercury, and which makes a triangle where it crosses the line of life, tells of a divorce. Parallel lines from Venus to Mars betray two love affairs carried on at the same time. A line from Venus which cuts the line of destiny means conjugal misery or misfortunes which come through a woman (or man). From the line of the heart, a line turned down to the line of the head, with a ray across it, indicates a miserable marriage, or deep griefs of the heart. Bars across the heart line show disappointments in love. A spot shows the loss of a loved one. A line from Mount Venus, which crosses over to Mount Apollo, shows a brilliant or fortunate chance of marriage, or great social success through the influence of friends.

Lines which cut across the line of life on Mount Terra indicate worry and trouble in early life. Conjugal unhappiness is shown by short angular lines running from the heart line to the head line. Wherever they cease to cut the heart line, the unhappiness will cease. The true divorce line should cut across the life, head and heart lines, and end on Mercury, cutting into the line of marriage that would be broken by the divorce, and form a triangle on the life line.

A line of destiny which arises from the Mount of the Moon, passes up to the heart line and mixes with it, and then goes on up to the Mount of Jupiter, infallibly indicates a rich and fortunate marriage. With spatulate hands, a person is apt to be constant in love. Apollo's subjects are frequently unfortunate in marriage, because they have too high an ideal. Mars' subjects often marry late in life, and with women of the Venus type.

A spot is thought to always denote a malady. If placed upon a line, it is the scar of a wound: thus, on the head line, it would mean a blow on the head. A white spot is, however, a harmless one.

Past and present signs: — We may distinguish between these in this way; a sign which is still visible, and yet seems to be more or less effaced, belongs to a past event. A sign which is clear and well colored is that of a present circumstance. And a line which seems only just visible, betraying itself just beneath the surface of the skin, is that of something to occur in the future.

There is considerable discussion among palmists as to which hand to read. I can only give you my experience, which has been this way: the left hand will show you the conditions of the child, the right will show what the person has become. You will notice a great difference between the two hands; but the right can be depended on to give the correct results of the past, present and future. But bear in mind, both hands should be studied before passing on an important event. The left hand will show hereditary conditions, the right will show if you have overcome them. Remember always, we have the power to change our life, if we so will. Blind forces can rule us only when we are in the dark. Let us be wise. Remember always the old adage: "The wise man rules his stars, the fool is ruled by them."

CHAPTER XXX.

Palmistry, and Its Relations to the Signs of the Zodiac.

Modern palmistry owes its growth chiefly to the work of Capt. DeArpentigny and Adrien Desbarrolles. The first published his Cheirognomy in 1843; and the latter his Mysteries of the Hand, in 1859. The most elaborate works hitherto published in English are the Manual of Cheirosophy, by Ed. Heron Allen, and Language of the Hand, by Cheiro. The great deficiency in all of these works is in the lack of complete engravings, and also in the lack of a thorough knowledge of physiology, astrology and phrenology on the part of these authors. From this latter cause, they made many mistakes in giving meanings.

THE SIGNS OF THE HAND.

We have sought to avoid these in the present work, and make all its deductions in harmony with those of the physical structure which govern alike the limbs and hands of all animals. We have diligently studied all these before drawing our final conclusions. The chart of the hand exhibits the general relations of each part to the planets, and to the months of the year. As the twelve signs of the Zodiac, so each phalange of the fingers is under the influence of its own months. I have found this to be true, and by the following method can tell the month a person is born in seven times out of ten:

The first phalange of the first finger is seen to be thus under the influence of Aries and the month of April.

The second phalange, of Taurus and the month of May.

The third, of Gemini and the month of June.

First phalange of second finger, Capricorn, month of January.

The second, Aquarius, month of February.

The third, Pisces, month of March.

First phalange of the third finger, Cancer, month of July.

Second, Leo, month of August.

Third, Virgo, month of September.

First phalange of fourth finger, Libra, month of October.

Second phalange, Scorpio, month of November.

Third, Sagittarius, month of December.

In looking over the different works on the Signs of the Zodiac, you will at once see how intimately related are palmistry and astrology. Now to illustrate:

People born in the sign Aries are quick and keen to perceive, and are noted for their good sense.

People born in Taurus are slow in motion, and slow to gain knowledge, as they have not a keen perception; they have to study hard for what they get.

Those born in Gemini are noted for their continuous search after wisdom and culture.

The Capricorn people are noted for their persistent efforts, and for their dignified and sober life.

The Aquarius people are noted for their business ability, especially their desire for possessions.

Those born in Pisces are noted for their desire to be sociable and conservative qualities.

The Cancer people are fond of the beautiful and artistic, and will always manage to dress well and in taste.

Those born in Leo show adaptability for business, but as a rule are not very industrious.

Virgo's people have a great deal of formality, and are great planners.

In Libra, the people are noted for their great inspiration and clairvoyant ability, and when well developed, are lovers of fair play and justice.

Persons born in Scorpio are noted for their versatility and their love for education; a fine sign.

The people in Sagittarius are, as a rule, fine appearing, with good expression, and rather venturesome when performing a duty.

Now, observe your two charts together, (Nos. 1 and 6). We have three sets of phalanges in the fingers, the material, reasoning and intuitive, four of each. Each set makes a polarity in the Zodiac; thus, Aries, Cancer, Capricorn, Libra. Now the set of phalanges which are the better developed will give you the polarity of months, and the one phalange of the four which is the strongest developed will give the month. The signs are modified so much sometimes by planetary conditions as to change this rule. My percentage of success in telling the right month has been about seven times in ten; in getting the right polarity, nine times out of ten. This has no especial value, only in proving the influence of astrology in building the hand and brain.

The Signs of the Zodiac have also their polarity in the brain. Study Chart No. 13, and note that in one born in June, or Gemini, the faculties of culture, music, wealth and art, would be the more highly developed; but Gemini must always borrow its art from Pisces, and Pisces will borrow its culture from Gemini. And so of all the others; that is, art will always be strongest in Pisces, and culture in Gemini.

The hand has also its relations to the geography of the earth. Thus, the top of the hand and the fingers are related to the north; the base of the hand, south; the thumb side, to the east, and the percussion side, to the west. The Southern people and races have been ruled by their feelings; the Northern

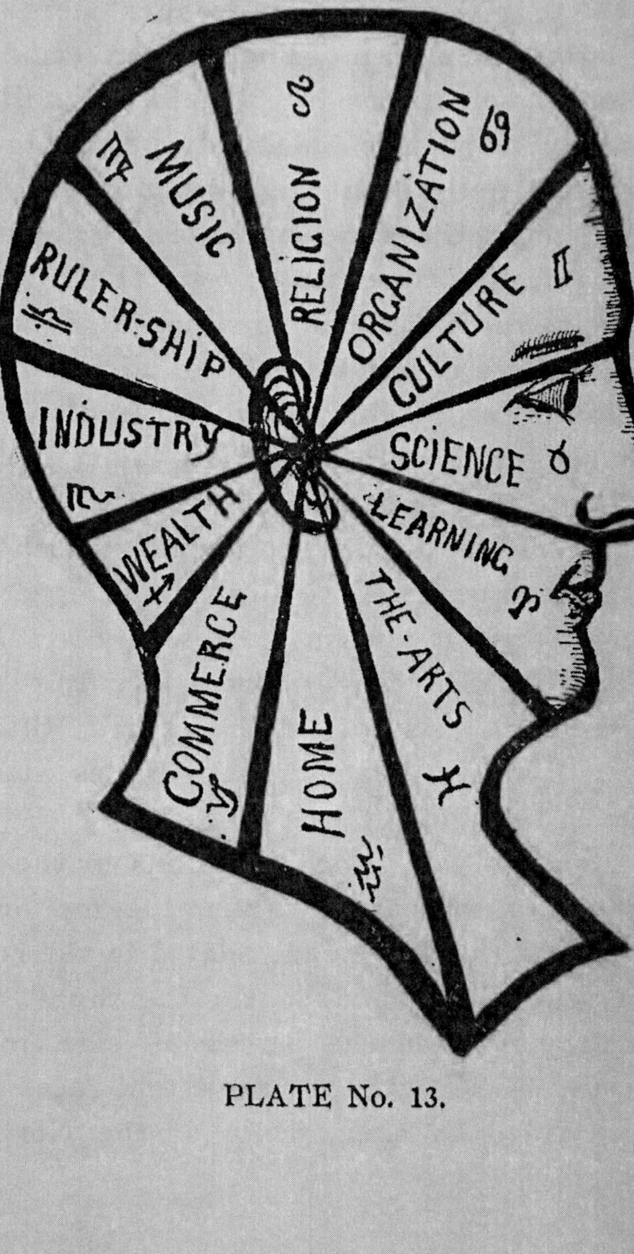
MUSIC
RELIGION
ORGANIZATION
RULER-SHIP
CULTURE
INDUSTRY
SCIENCE
LEARNING
WEALTH
COMMERCE
HOME
THE-ARTS

PLATE No. 13.

races have worked out the most details of science and industry, things dependent upon the fingers.

We may consider the base of the hand female, while the top of the hand is male. The faculties of love and emotion are stronger in the female, while intelligence and knowledge are male attributes; therefore, if a man's hand be stronger at the base, the female attributes will predominate, and vice versa. Also, one is considered to be more fortunate in life if he follows the development of the hand in locating: thus, if the southern part is the strongest, go south, etc.

The professions or work, which people will be apt to choose, and that for which they are fitted by nature, may be judged by the types of the hand, and the development of its mounts.

The farmer should have a mixture of the spatulate and square type of hand, with a good Mount of the Moon, and a strong line of life.

The horticulturist will have a high Mount of Venus and of the Moon, with long spatulate fingers to give them activity and capacity for details. Venus gives the love of flowers and plants.

An architect will show a good Mount of Jupiter, a strong line of Apollo and hard hands of the square type, with broad fingers.

A sculptor will be marked with a thick hard hand, in which are high Mounts of Mars, Venus and the Moon, with square or broad fingers.

The painter, of course, would have the artistic, or conical hand, but he may also have the mixed type of fingers, with large Mounts of Venus and Apollo.

The astronomer has well developed Mounts of the Moon, Mercury and Saturn. With these, he requires the long knotty fingers, to be attracted to the necessary work of mathematical calculation.

The physician will show us a square hand with rays upon the Mount of Mercury, and a clear line of Apollo. If a surgeon, he should have a hard hand and spatulate fingers, and a large Mount of Mars.

Musicians whose work is instrumental will play best if they have spatulate fingers, with a high Mount of Saturn, short nails, well developed back of thumb, full joints, a prominent Mount of Venus and of the Moon, and a good line of Apollo.

For vocal music, the person may have small fingers, with mixed types, and a good Mount of Venus.

The actor will display square or spatulate fingers, with the third one long. The Mount of Venus will be well developed, and the head line forked at the end. The heart line turns upward toward the Mount of Mercury, which is well developed, and often is found connecting Mars and Apollo.

Rulers and statesmen should have the square type of hand, with a large Mount of Jupiter, with logical joints; they will have a love of progress, wisdom and justice, united to a love of order and stability.

Commercial men and merchants have rather soft hands, the fingers thick and smooth, the thumb large and conic, and the hand seeming to close easier than it opens.

To the mixed type of hands belongs the talent for dealing best with people, as merchants and administrators of justice.

The gambler or speculator will show a long

slender hand, with the three first fingers on the hand nearly of the same length, with a small Mount of Jupiter and Saturn.

A PROPER IMPRESS OF THE HAND.

To successfuly take impression of the hand use a small piece of gum camphor, place in dish, and light with match; this makes a very black smoke. Pass a sheet of unruled paper over smoke until well blacked, —or you can use a lamp. Lay paper on table, and firmly press the hand down on smoked surface, with the fingers slightly apart. Pass a pencil around the entire hand; be careful to get a perfect outline of each finger and thumb. Remove the hand, then pour alcohol over the impression, as a fixitive, let it evaporate. In this way, secure a good impression of *both* hands.

CHAPTER XXXI.

Physiognomy.

I would also encourage the student to take up the study of Physiognomy, which you will find of value to you in a thousand ways. I will give a few points only in this work.

A person with thick lips is warm hearted, has a strong love nature, is fond of kissing, and, as a rule, lacks in firmness. Thin lips show the opposite qualities, with a tendency to fault finding and scolding. The lips are ruled by Venus, and show the higher sex center in the body.

The nose is ruled by Mars, and will correspond with the thumb, as a rule. A large, well developed nose shows great will power; a small, flat nose, inferior will power. A nose with a scooped out appearance in the center will show a timid, childish nature, but when the center rises, mountain shape, you have an aggressive, stubborn, determined character to deal with.

The eye, if round or nearly so, shows a pure, unselfish, spiritual nature, but if long and narrow, giving a sleepy appearance, selfishness or sensuality will predominate. Compare the bird and cat.

The long, narrow forehead shows greater mental concentration, but little originality; the broad, high forehead, imitation and originality, and intuition strong; but if the forehead be low and also slanting, a lack of originality and intuition.

A large, wide ear shows greater genius than a small, narrow ear. The large ear also shows generosity; the small ear, stinginess.

A strong, wide chin shows stability, firmness and great heart action. In the motive temperament this chin predominates. The small, slanting chin shows a lack of stability and poor heart action.

The skin on the face should be studied the same as the skin of the hand.

Every thought passing in the mind is depicted on the countenance. Try as hard as you will to repress this effect, the skilled faceologist can read you. Oh, for the day when we will all be skilled in the science of

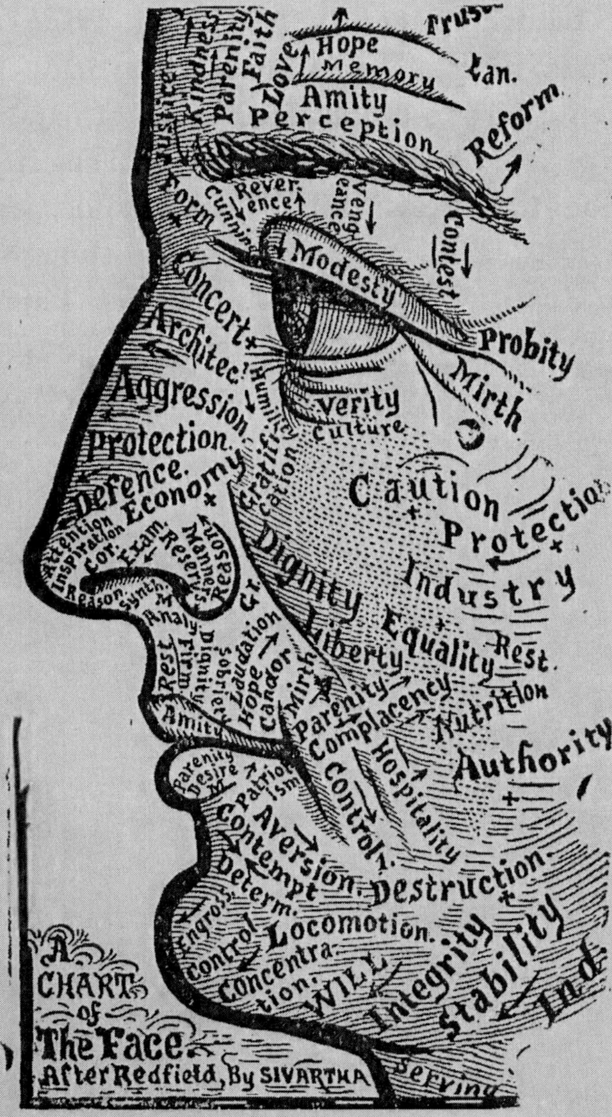
Justice
Kindness
Parenity
Faith
Love
Hope
Memory
Trust
Lan.
Amity
Perception
Reform
Form
Reverence
Contest
Modesty
Concert
Architec.
Probity
Mirth
Aggression
Verity
Culture
Protection
Defence.
Economy
Caution
Protection
Attention
Inspiration
Cor.
Exam.
Reserve
Reason
Synth.
Industry
Dignity
Equality
Rest.
Liberty
Rest
Firm
Laudation
Hope
Candor
Mirth
Parenity
Complacency
Nutrition
Amity
Authority
Parenity
Desire
Patriotism
Control
Hospitality
Aversion
Contempt
Determ.
Destruction
Control
Locomotion
Concentration.
WILL
Integrity
Stability
Ind.
Serving
A CHART of The Face.
After Redfield, By SIVARTHA

PLATE No. 14.

character reading. It is the means to the end of banishing deceit, hypocrisy, lying, and a thousand other evils from the world; for all men desire to be thought well of, and when they learn this science, they will see it is the thoughts they think that build beautiful or ugly faces. Think beautiful thoughts and you can have a beautiful face. Think evil thoughts, and you will spoil the most finely chiseled countenance the Creator ever formed.

CHAPTER XXXII.

Conclusion.

Now, dear reader, this will complete the Science of Palmistry, which you will find, if thoroughly learned, will be all you require to become a firstclass character reader. The fortune telling part of this science I purposely leave out in all its multitude of detail, giving only the main points which can be easily learned and understood.

We are coming to recognize more and more that we are the makers and rulers of our own destinies, and the palmist who can tell us how to build up our own self confidence and teach us to stand alone is of far more value than he who predicts a fortune left by some dead friend,—which we should scorn to accept, and we truly would scorn to accept it, if we could once realize the beauty of sturdy manhood and womanhood. Let us learn to be gods, in very truth, and spurn all props that would sustain us in our faltering weakness, and with the power born of knowledge go forth in the battle of life, to stand or fall on our own merits.

> Oh, the glory of walking apart,
> One with God in the infinite march,
> Without props, and with none to atone,
> Dependent on self worth alone.

JULIAN W. SMITH,

..ASTROLOGER..

Full Life Readings containing from 20 to 30 pages of manuscript telling past, present and future events and conditions of your life, with instructions how to shape your course in life to bring about the best results. Price for above Horoscope $2.00; $1.00 additional for each year's exact business information. Send date of birth, hour when possible, and the state or country where you were born and sex. Five questions answered by Horary-Astrology $1.00. Send exact date, day and hour when asking question or questions.

Address, JULIAN W. SMITH,

P. O. Box 945,

TACOMA, WASH